Hot and Spicy

Bloomsbury Books
London

This edition published 1995 by Bloomsbury Books,
an imprint of The Godfrey Cave Group,
42 Bloomsbury Street, London, WC1B 3QJ.

ISBN 1 85471 562 3

Printed and bound in Great Britain.

Hot and Spicy

Contents

Sichuan Peppercorn Lamb 7
Lamb Chili Verde 8
Lamb Tikka 9
Potatoes with a Spiced Lamb Stuffing 10
Moroccan Spiced Stew 11
Chili Lamb Tortillas 12
Lamb Dhansak 13
Hot and Sweet Soup with Seafood Dumplings 14
Skewered Beef with Julienned Papaya 15
Veal and Apricot Brochettes Tikka-Style 16
Stir-Fried Ginger Beef with Watercress 17
Sichuan Stir-Fried Veal and Crunchy Vegetables 18
Lemon-Cardamom Braised Beef 19
Spicy Minced Beef Baked in Corn Bread 20
Gingered Prawns on Black Beans 21
Seven-Spice Stew with Mussels, Squid and Prawns 22
Grilled Prawns with Tomato-Ginger Sauce 23
Vegetable Stew, East Indian-Style 24
Seafood Chili with Peppers 25
Plaice Curry 26
Prawn Creole 27
Southwest Gumbo 28
Mexican Chicken Stew with Chilies 29
Java Lamb Curry with Tamarind 30
Chunky Beef Chili 31
Boiled Yam with Hot Pepper Sauce 32
Spiced Red Cabbage 33
Chestnut-Stuffed Sweet Potatoes with Chili Sauce 34
Potato, Carrot and Cauliflower Curry 35
Saffron and Potato Stew with Rouille 36
Spiced Steak Phyllo Boats 37
Spiced Peanut Dip with Crudité Skewers 38
Sweet and Spicy Sweetcorn Salad 39
Curried Cabbage Coleslaw 40
Curried Black-Eyed Peas 41

Black Bean, Rice and Pepper Salad 42
Saffron Chicken with Yogurt 43
Roast Gingered Turkey Breast 44
Turkey Satays with Peanut Sauce 45
Turkey Curry with Puréed Yams 46
Turkey and Green Chili Enchiladas 47
Chopped Turkey with Lime and Coriander 48
Chicken and Mango Brochettes with Honey-Lime Sauce 49
Devilled Mushroom Tartlets 50
Middle-Eastern Spiced Carrot Salad 51
Spiced Fillet of Beef 52
Ginger and Coriander Fish Balls 53
Mexican Beef Brochettes 54
Red Pork 55
Mexican Pork 56
Kofta with Curry Sauce and Cucumber 57
Spiced Chili Beef with Yogurt 58
Haddock Enchiladas with Chili Sauce 59
Chili and Lime Avocado Dip 60
Spicy Chicken Wings 61
Curry Fettuccine with Chicken and Avocado 62
Chicken with Orange and Onion 63
Leg of Lamb in Spiced Apple Sauce 64
Moussaka 65
Spicy Beef Salad 66
Lamb Paprika 67
Barbecued Veal with Spicy Orange Sauce 68
Hamburgers with Spicy Ketchup Sauce 69
Spit-Roasted Savoury Chicken 70
Yogurt Chicken Drumsticks 71

Sichuan Peppercorn Lamb

Serves 4

Working time: about 30 minutes

Total time: about 45 minutes

Calories 290
Protein 32g
Cholesterol 80mg
Total fat 14g
Saturated fat 5g
Sodium 135mg

4	loin chops, trimmed	4
2 tsp	Sichuan peppercorns	2 tsp
1 tbsp	soy sauce	1 tbsp
1 tbsp	dry sherry	1 tbsp
125 g	French beans, topped and tailed, cut in half	4 oz
½ tbsp	safflower oil	½ tbsp

1 tbsp	finely chopped spring onions	1 tbsp
1	large carrot, peeled and julienned	1
1	sweet red pepper, seeded, deribbed and julienned	1
	green ends of spring onions, sliced for garnish	

Heat a heavy pan over medium heat and toast the peppercorns by stirring them for about 30 seconds. Grind them to a fine powder, then mix 1 teaspoon of ground peppercorns together with the soya sauce and sherry in a shallow dish. Place the chops in the dish, turn them to coat them and leave to marinate for 20 minutes; turn them once during this time.

Meanwhile, parboil the French beans in boiling water for 3 minutes. Drain and rinse them under cold running water. Drain again and set them aside. Preheat the grill to high.

Remove the chops from the dish and discard the marinade. Dust the chops with the remaining crushed peppercorns, and pin the flap of lean meat to the eye of each chop with a cocktail stick. Grill the chops for 4 to 6 minutes on each side for rare to medium meat.

While the chops are cooking, stir-fry the vegetables. In a wok or frying pan, heat the oil until it is hot but not smoking. Add the chopped spring onions and fry them for 30 seconds, stirring constantly, then add the julienned carrot and pepper and the beans. Stir fry all the vegetables for 2 minutes, then serve them immediately with the grilled chops. Garnish the chops with the spring onion slices.

Lamb Chili Verde

Serves 6

Working time:
about 30
minutes

Total time:
about 2 hours
and 30 minutes
(includes
soaking)

Calories
360
Protein
37g
Cholesterol
75mg
Total fat
12g
Saturated fat
5g
Sodium
185mg

750 g	lean lamb trimmed and cut in pieces	1½ lb	2	fresh hot green chili peppers, seeded and chopped	2
200 g	dried pinto beans, picked over	7 oz	750 g	green tomatoes, skinned, seeded and coarsely chopped	1½ lb
1 tbsp	safflower oil	1 tbsp	2 tbsp	dark brown sugar	2 tbsp
1	onion, finely chopped	1	½ tsp	cumin seeds	½ tsp
¼ tsp	salt	¼ tsp	1	cucumber, peeled, seeded and coarsely chopped	1
	freshly ground black pepper				
35 cl	chicken stock	12 fl oz	30 g	Cheddar cheese, grated	1 oz
2	garlic cloves, finely chopped	2			

Rinse the pinto beans under cold running water, then put them into a large saucepan well covered with water. Discard any beans that float to the surface. Cover the pan, leaving the lid ajar, and slowly bring the liquid to the boil. Boil the beans for 2 minutes, then turn off the heat and soak, covered, for at least 1 hour.

Heat the oil in a large, saucepan over medium-high heat. Add the lamb pieces and sauté them for about 3 minutes. Reduce the heat to medium and add the onion, the salt and some pepper. Cook until the onion is translucent—about 3 minutes. Add the garlic and cook for 1 minute more. Drain the beans and add them to the pan. Stir in the chili peppers, all but 125 g (4 oz) of the tomatoes, the stock, brown sugar, cumin seeds and ½ litre (16 fl oz) of water. Bring to a simmer and cook, covered, for 1 hour. Add the cucumber and remaining tomatoes and simmer for a further 15 minutes, then remove the lid and simmer until the beans are tender. Serve with the grated cheese on top.

Lamb Tikka

Serves 2

Working time:
about 30
minutes

Total time:
about 5 hours
(includes
marinating)

Calories
255
Protein
32g
Cholesterol
75mg
Total fat
9g
Saturated fat
4g
Sodium
100mg

500 g	lean lamb, trimmed and cut into cubes	**1 lb**
2.5 cm	piece fresh ginger root, peeled and coarsely chopped	**1 inch**
2	garlic cloves, coarsely chopped	**2**
2	green chili peppers, seeded and coarsely chopped	**2**
2 tsp	cumin seeds	**2 tsp**

1 tsp	ground turmeric	**1 tsp**
½ tsp	ground fenugreek	**½ tsp**
12	mint leaves	**12**
15 cl	plain low-fat yogurt	**¼ pint**
1 tbsp	fresh lime juice	**1 tbsp**
2	star anise pods	**2**
350 g	fresh pineapple cut in chunks	**12 oz**

Put the meat in a bowl. In a blender or food processor, purée the ginger, garlic, chilies, cumin, turmeric, fenugreek and mint leaves. Add the yogurt and lime juice and blend to mix. Pour the purée over the meat, add the star anise and mix well to coat the meat thoroughly. Leave to marinate in a cool place for 4 to 6 hours, stirring occasionally.

Preheat the grill to hot. Thread the cubes of meat and pineapple alternately on to four metal kebab skewers; reserve the marinade. Place the kebabs on a grill rack and grill until the lamb is cooked but still slightly pink in the centre—10 to 15 minutes. Turn the skewers frequently and baste the meat with the reserved marinade while grilling.

Potatoes with a Spiced Lamb Stuffing

Serves 4	
Working time: about 40 minutes	
Total time: about 1 hour and 40 minutes	

Calories	270
Protein	14g
Cholesterol	25mg
Total fat	5g
Saturated fat	2g
Sodium	230mg

150 g	lean lamb, trimmed and minced	5 oz
8	even-sized potatoes, scrubbed	8
1	small onion, finely chopped	1
1	garlic clove, crushed	1
1 tbsp	raisins, rinsed and finely chopped	1 tbsp
1 tbsp	pine-nuts, roughly chopped	1 tbsp

1 tsp	ground cinnamon	1 tsp
½ tsp	ground allspice	½ tsp
½ tsp	ground turmeric	½ tsp
2 tbsp	tomato paste	2 tbsp
¼ tsp	salt	¼ tsp
	freshly ground black pepper	
6 tbsp	unsalted brown or chicken stock	6 tbsp
1 tbsp	crème fraîche	1 tbsp

Preheat the oven to 200°C (400°F or Mark 6).

Make a deep horizontal slit about one quarter of the way down each potato. Bake them in the oven for about 1 hour.

Meanwhile, make the stuffing. Lightly brush a non-stick frying pan with oil and heat it over medium heat. Stir-fry the onion until it is brown. Add the minced lamb and continue stir-frying until it changes colour, then add the garlic, raisins, pine-nuts, cinnamon, allspice, turmeric, tomato paste, salt and some freshly ground pepper. Stir for 1 minute, then add the stock and continue cooking the mixture for a further 5 minutes. Set the stuffing aside.

When the potatoes are cool enough to handle, slice off their tops and hollow out their insides with a teaspoon, taking care not to puncture their skins; leave a shell of about 5 mm (¼ inch) on each potato. Mash half of the scooped-out potato with the crème fraîche. Spoon the mashed potato into the potato shells, pressing down in the centre to make a well for the lamb stuffing. Fill the shells with the stuffing and return them to the oven to heat through—about 10 minutes. Serve immediately.

Moroccan Spiced Stew

Serves 4

Working time:
about 30
minutes

Total time:
about 1 hour
and 45
minutes

Calories
315
Protein
36g
Cholesterol
80mg
Total fat
14g
Saturated fat
4g
Sodium
175mg

500 g	lean lamb	1 lb	½ tsp	saffron threads	½ tsp
	trimmed and cut into cubes		½ tsp	ground ginger	½ tsp
½ tsp	safflower oil	½ tsp	¼ tsp	grated nutmeg	¼ tsp
350 g	pickling onions	12 oz	½	orange, grated rind and juice	½
45 cl	unsalted brown or	¾ pint	12	ready-to-eat stoned prunes	12
	chicken stock		30 g	blanched almonds	1 oz
1 tbsp	clear honey	1 tbsp	¼ tsp	salt	¼ tsp
1 tsp	ground cinnamon	1 tsp		freshly ground black pepper	

Heat the oil in a non-stick frying pan over medium-high heat and sauté the onions until they are golden-brown—about 5 minutes. Transfer them to a bowl and set them aside.

Add the lamb cubes to the frying pan and brown them for 2 to 3 minutes. Transfer them to a large, heavy-bottomed saucepan or fireproof casserole.

Pour off any fat from the frying pan, then add the stock and bring it to the boil, stirring with a wooden spoon to dislodge any deposits from the bottom of the pan. Pour the boiling stock over the lamb. Add the honey, cinnamon, saffron, ginger and nutmeg to the casserole, cover and simmer for 30 minutes.

Add the onions, orange rind and juice to the lamb and simmer for a further 30 minutes. Finally add the prunes, almonds and salt, season with pepper and simmer, uncovered, for 15 minutes

Chili Lamb Tortillas

Serves 4		Calories 385
Working time: about 50 minutes		Protein 28g
Total time: about 3 hours and 30 minutes (includes soaking)		Cholesterol 24mg
		Total fat 12g
		Saturated fat 4g
		Sodium 240mg

250 g	lean lamb, diced	**8 oz**
175 g	dried borlotti beans	**6 oz**
1 tbsp	safflower oil	**1 tbsp**
2	onions, chopped	**2**
1	sweet red pepper, chopped	**1**
1	garlic clove, chopped	**1**
2 tbsp	tomato paste	**2 tbsp**
3	tomatoes, skinned, seeded and chopped	**3**

1	green chili pepper, seeded and chopped	**1**
15 cl	unsalted brown stock	**$\frac{1}{4}$ pint**
$\frac{1}{4}$ tsp	salt	**$\frac{1}{4}$ tsp**
	freshly ground black pepper	
	Tortilla dough	
90 g	plain flour	**3 oz**
$\frac{1}{8}$ tsp	salt	**$\frac{1}{8}$ tsp**
15 g	hard white vegetable fat	**$\frac{1}{2}$ oz**

Rinse the beans. Boil them, well covered with water, for 2 minutes then soak for 1 hour. Rinse, cover well with water, boil for 10 minutes, then simmer until tender. Drain and rinse.

To make the tortillas, sift the flour and salt into a bowl and rub in the fat until the mixture resembles fine breadcrumbs. Add 3 to 4 tablespoons warm water and mix in a stiff dough. Knead on a floured surface until smooth. Shape into four balls and roll into 18 cm (7 inch) circles.

Heat a heavy frying pan and fry the tortillas, in turn, until pale brown on both sides. Place each tortilla over an inverted dariole mould so that they will cool and harden in a cupped shape.

Heat the oil in a sauté pan. Add the lamb and stir until sealed. Add the onions, red pepper and garlic and sauté gently until the onions soften. Add the tomatoes, chili pepper, tomato paste and stock; season. Cover and cook for ten minutes. Add the beans and heat through, then keep warm. Preheat the oven to 180°C (350°F or Mark 4).

Reheat the tortillas for ten minutes in the oven. Fill with chili and serve.

Lamb Dhansak

Serves 4

Working time:
about 50 minutes

Total time:
about 10 hours
(includes soaking)

Calories
285
Protein
35g
Cholesterol
75mg
Total fat
8g
Saturated fat
4g
Sodium
340mg

500 g	lean lamb, cubed	**1 lb**
1	large onion, finely chopped	**1**
2 tsp	ground coriander	**2 tsp**
2 tsp	ground cumin	**2 tsp**
1 tsp	ground cinnamon	**1 tsp**
1 tsp	ground cardamom	**1 tsp**
1 tsp	ground turmeric	**1 tsp**
1 tsp	black peppercorns	**1 tsp**
20 cl	plain low-fat yogurt	**7 fl oz**
2	garlic cloves, crushed	**2**
2	green chili peppers, chopped	**2**
2.5 cm	piece ginger root, grated	**1 inch**
250 g	mixed lentils, soaked for 8 hours or overnight, drained	**8 oz**
350 g	aubergine, cubed	**12 oz**
250 g	butternut squash, cubed	**8 oz**
350 g	tomatoes, finely chopped	**12 oz**
150 g	fresh spinach, washed and torn into small pieces	**5 oz**
½ tsp	salt	**½ tsp**
3 tbsp	fresh coriander, chopped	**3 tbsp**

Brush a large fireproof casserole with oil. Add the onion and cook, stirring, until softened. Stir in the lamb, ground spices and peppercorns, then add 1 tablespoon of the yogurt. Cook over high heat, stirring until the yogurt is absorbed. Add the rest of the yogurt, gradually, stirring constantly until all the yogurt is absorbed.

Stir in the garlic, chili peppers and ginger, and cook for 1 minute. Add the lentils, aubergine, squash, tomatoes and spinach and add just enough water to cover. Bring to the boil, then reduce the heat to low, cover and simmer until the lamb is tender. Add more water as necessary. 10 minutes before the end of cooking, add the salt and fresh coriander.

Lift out the meat and about half of the vegetable and lentil mixture with a slotted spoon and set it aside. Mash the lentil and vegetable mixture left in the pan, then reincorporate the meat and the rest of the mixture and gently reheat it. Serve.

Hot and Sweet Soup with Seafood Dumplings

Serves 8

Working time:
1 hour

Total time:
about 1 hour
and 15
minutes

Calories
135
Protein
17g
Cholesterol
75mg
Total fat
3g
Saturated fat
1g
Sodium
240mg

250 g	chopped lean pork	8 oz	1	egg white, beaten	1
250 g	fresh prawns, peeled and finely chopped	8 oz	2 litres	unsalted chicken stock	2 litres
			2 tsp	sweet chili sauce	2 tsp
250 g	white crab meat, picked over	8 oz	12.5 cl	fresh lemon juice	4 fl oz
2	spring onions	2	250 g	small cantaloupe melon balls	8 oz
1½ tsp	ginger root, finely chopped	1½ tsp	¼ tsp	salt	¼ tsp

Combine the pork, prawns, crab meat, spring onions, ginger and egg white in a large bowl. Shape heaped teaspoonfuls of the mixture into dumplings about 2.5 cm (1 inch) in diameter.

Pour the stock into a large pan and bring it to the boil. Reduce the heat to a simmer and add the chili sauce and four tablespoons of the lemon juice. Gently drop half of the dumplings into the hot liquid and simmer them for 5 minutes. Remove the dumplings with a slotted spoon and set them aside. Drop the remaining dumplings into the liquid and simmer for 5 minutes. When the second batch is done, return the first batch to the pan. Heat through, then add the melon balls, the salt and the remaining lemon juice. Serve in individual bowls.

Skewered Beef with Julienned Papaya

1 kg	rump steak, trimmed	2 lb	2	spring onions, white parts only, thinly sliced	2
2	underripe papayas seeded and julienned	2	1½ tbsp	ginger root, chopped	1½ tbsp
2 tbsp	fresh lime juice	2 tbsp	3	garlic cloves, chopped	3
32	cherry tomatoes, halved	32	2	dried red chili peppers, chopped	2
2	spring onions, green parts only, thinly sliced	2	3 tbsp	peanut butter	3 tbsp
2 tbsp	crushed unsalted roasted peanuts	2 tbsp	4 tbsp	plain low-fat yogurt	4 tbsp
	Spicy peanut marinade		2 tbsp	dry white wine	2 tbsp
			2 tbsp	fresh lime juice	2 tbsp
2½ tbsp	low-sodium soy sauce	2½ tbsp	1 tbsp	honey	1 tbsp

Combine the soy sauce with the spring onions, ginger, garlic, and chili peppers in a large bowl. Let the mixture stand for 1 minute, then whisk in the remaining marinade ingredients.

Slice the beef into thin strips and toss into the marinade and allow it to sit for 1 hour at room temperature.

Meanwhile, mix the papaya julienne and the lime juice in a bowl and refrigerate.

Preheat the grill for 10 minutes.

Insert a wooden skewer through a tomato half, then thread it through a strip of beef; finish with another tomato half. Repeat for the remaining tomatoes and beef. Brush with any remaining marinade.

Cook the meat in two batches until it begins to brown—4 to 6 minutes then transfer the skewers to a serving platter.

Sprinkle the meat with the sliced spring onion greens and crushed peanuts, and serve the chilled papaya or mango alongside.

15

Veal and Apricot Brochettes Tikka-Style

Serves 4

Working time: about 30 minutes

Total time: about 6 hours and 45 minutes (includes marinating)

Calories 180
Protein 20g
Cholesterol 75mg
Total fat 5g
Saturated fat 2g
Sodium 240mg

350 g	veal topside, trimmed and cubed	**12 oz**
60 g	dried apricots, halved	**2 oz**
250 g	courgettes, cut into chunks	**8 oz**
	lime wedges or slices for garnish	
	Spicy yogurt marinade	
30 cl	plain low-fat yogurt	**½ pint**
1	small onion, chopped	1
1	garlic clove, chopped	1
1 cm	fresh ginger root, peeled	**½ inch**

1	lime, juice only	1
2	cardamom pods	2
1	small dried red chili pepper	1
4	cloves	4
6	black peppercorns	6
5 mm	piece cinnamon stick	**¼ inch**
1tsp	grated nutmeg	1 tsp
¼ tsp	coriander seeds	¼ tsp
¼ tsp	cumin seeds	¼ tsp
¼ tsp	salt	¼ tsp

Combine the yogurt, onion, garlic, ginger and lime juice in a food processor and blend until quite smooth. Strain into a bowl.

Break open the cardamom pods and put the seeds in a mortar. Add the chili pepper, cloves, peppercorns, cinnamon stick, nutmeg, coriander seeds and cumin seeds. Pound until fine. Add the spices and the salt to the yogurt mixture and stir well. Add the cubes of veal and the apricots, and coat them in the mixture. Refrigerate the marinate for 6 hours.

Preheat the grill. Thread the veal cubes, apricots and courgettes on to four or eight skewers, shaking off and reserving excess marinade. Grill the kebabs for about 15 minutes, turning them to cook and brown evenly.

While the kebabs are cooking, strain the marinade through a fine sieve into a small, heavy-bottomed saucepan. Heat the marinade through very gently; do not boil. Serve the kebabs garnished with lime wedges or slices and pass the heated marinade sauce separately.

Stir-Fried Ginger Beef with Watercress

Serves 4

Working time:
about 20
minutes

Total time:
about 1 hour
10 minutes

Calories
195
Protein
21g
Cholesterol
55mg
Total fat
7g
Saturated fat
2g
Sodium
440mg

500 g	rumpsteak, trimmed and sliced into thin strips	1 lb	4 tbsp	unsalted chicken stock	4 tbsp
½ tbsp	groundnut oil	½ tbsp	1 tsp	cornflour	1 tsp
1	bunch watercress, trimmed, washed and dried	1	1 tsp	sugar	1 tsp
	Ginger marinade			**Cucumber salad**	
5 cm	fresh ginger root, chopped	2 inch	500 g	cucumbers, seeded and cut into thick strips	1 lb
1 tbsp	chili paste, or 1 tsp hot red pepper flakes	1 tbsp	¼ tsp	salt	¼ tsp
4 tbsp	dry sherry	4 tbsp	4 tbsp	rice vinegar or distilled white vinegar	4 tbsp
			1 tsp	dark sesame oil	1 tsp

Combine all of the marinade ingredients in a bowl. Add the beef and toss it well; cover the bowl and marinate the meat for 1 hour at room temperature.

Combine the cucumbers, salt, vinegar and sesame oil in a bowl. Refrigerate the salad.

When the marinating time is up, drain the beef, reserving the marinade. Heat the oil in a large, non-stick frying pan or a well-seasoned wok over high heat. Add the beef and stir-fry it until it is well browned—about 2 minutes. Add the reserved marinade; stir constantly until the sauce thickens—about 1 minute. Add the watercress and toss the mixture quickly. Serve the stir-fried beef and watercress immediately, accompanied by the chilled cucumber salad.

Sichuan Stir-Fried Veal and Crunchy Vegetables

Serves 4

Working time:
about 40
minutes

Total time:
about 2 hours
and 40
minutes

Calories
300
Protein
30g
Cholesterol
110mg
Total fat
14g
Saturated fat
3g
Sodium
215mg

500 g	veal escalopes, trimmed, and cut diagonally into stips	1 lb
4 tbsp	low-sodium soy sauce	4 tbsp
4 tbsp	sake or dry sherry	4 tbsp
2	dried red chili peppers, finely chopped	2
2 tbsp	safflower oil	2 tbsp
6	spring onions, sliced diagonally	6
2.5 cm	fresh ginger root, cut into very fine julienne	1 inch

1 to 2	garlic cloves, crushed	1 to 2
125 g	whole baby sweet corns	4 oz
250 g	carrots, julienned	8 oz
125 g	cauliflower florets	4 oz
125 g	French beans,	4 oz
30 cl	unsalted chicken	½ pint
1 tbsp	tomato paste	1 tbsp
1½ tbsp	cornflour, mixed with 1 tbsp cold water	1½ tbsp
	freshly ground black pepper	
1 tbsp	sesame oil	1 tbsp

Combine the veal, 2 tablespoons each of the soy sauce and sake, and the chilies. Marinate for 2 hours, turning occasionally.

Gently heat a wok and pour in the safflower oil. Add the spring onions, ginger and garlic, and stir-fry for 30 seconds to flavour the oil. Add the veal and its marinade and stir-fry until all the strips have changed colour. Remove the veal and flavourings with a slotted spoon and set aside; do not discard the oil.

Add the baby sweetcorn to the pan and stir-

fry, tossing constantly, for 2 minutes, then add the carrots, cauliflower and beans, and stir-fry for 2 more minutes. Return the veal and flavourings to the pan and mix. Push the contents to the sides and pour the stock into the centre. Stir in the tomato paste, remaining soy sauce and sake, the cornflour mixture and some pepper, and bring to the boil to thicken. Put the veal and vegetables in the sauce and stir to coat. Serve with the sesame oil sprinkled over the top.

18

Lemon-Cardamom Braised Beef

Serves 8
Working time:
about 1 hour
Total time:
about 3 hours

Calories
240
Protein
29g
Cholesterol
80mg
Total fat
8g
Saturated fat
3g
Sodium
290mg

1.5 kg	topside of beef, trimmed	**3 lb**	**½ tsp**	ground cardamom	**½ tsp**
2 tsp	safflower oil	**2 tsp**	**½ tsp**	salt	**½ tsp**
2	onions, cut into eighths	**2**	**2¼ tsp**	fresh lemon juice	**2¼ tsp**
2	sticks celery, coarsely chopped	**2**	**1 tbsp**	Dijon mustard	**1 tbsp**
2	garlic cloves, chopped	**2**		freshly ground black pepper	
¾ litre	unsalted brown stock	**1¼ pint**	**500 g**	carrots	**1 lb**
12.5 cl	dry white wine	**4 fl oz**	**500 g**	courgettes, halved lengthwise	**1 lb**
1	lemon, rind only, cut into strips	**1**		and sliced diagonally	

Heat the oil in a shallow fireproof casserole or a large, deep sauté pan over high heat. Sear the beef until browned all over — 10 to 15 minutes. Tuck the onions, celery and garlic round the beef, and add the stock, wine, lemon rind, ¼ teaspoon of the cardamom, and ¼ teaspoon of the salt. Bring to the boil, then lower the heat to a slow simmer. Cover the pan, leaving the lid slightly ajar, and braise for 1 hour. Turn the beef over and cook until tender—1½ hours. Transfer to a carving board and cover loosely with aluminium foil.

Strain the cooking liquid into a saucepan. Whisk in 1½ tablespoons of the lemon juice, the mustard, plenty of pepper, the remaining cardamom, and salt. Simmer until it is reduced to 30 cl (½ pint).

Peel the carrots and cut them with a roll cut.

Pour water into a saucepan 2.5 cm (1 inch) deep. Set a vegetable steamer in the pan and bring to the boil. Add the carrots, cover, and steam until they begin to soften. Transfer to a large frying pan over medium-high heat. Add the courgettes, the remaining lemon juice, 12.5 cl (4 fl oz) of the sauce and plenty of pepper. Cook until most of the liquid has evaporated and the vegetables are glazed.

Slice the beef thinly and arrange on a serving platter with the vegetables. Reheat the remaining sauce and pour it over the beef.

Spicy Minced Beef Baked in Corn Bread

Serves 4

Working time:
about 25
minutes

Total time:
about 1 hour

Calories
395
Protein
28g
Cholesterol
55mg
Total fat
10g
Saturated fat
3g
Sodium
325mg

500 g	topside of beef, trimmed, minced, and crumbled	1 lb
1	onion, chopped	1
$\frac{1}{2}$	sweet green pepper, seeded, deribbed and diced	$\frac{1}{2}$
3	garlic cloves, thinly sliced	3
1 tsp	chili powder	1 tsp
1 tsp	dry mustard	1 tsp
$\frac{1}{4}$ tsp	cayenne pepper	$\frac{1}{4}$ tsp
400 g	canned whole tomatoes,	14 oz
1	sugar	1

6 tbsp	red wine vinegar	6 tbsp
$\frac{1}{8}$ tsp	salt	$\frac{1}{8}$ tsp
Corn bread		
80 g	corn meal	$2\frac{3}{4}$ oz
90 g	plain flour	3 oz
1 tbsp	sugar	1 tbsp
$1\frac{1}{2}$ tsp	baking powder	$1\frac{1}{2}$ tsp
$\frac{1}{2}$ tsp	chili powder	$\frac{1}{2}$ tsp
1 tbsp	safflower oil	1 tbsp
17.5 cl	semi-skimmed milk	6 fl oz
1	egg white	1

Heat a non-stick frying pan over medium-high heat. Combine the beef, onion, green pepper, garlic, chili powder, mustard and cayenne pepper in the pan. Stir the mixture, until the beef is cooked through. Add the tomatoes, sugar, vinegar and salt, crushing the tomatoes; cook the mixture until most of the liquid has evaporated. Set it aside.

Preheat the oven to 230°C (450°F or Mark 8).

To make the corn bread, sift the cornmeal, flour, sugar, baking powder and chili powder into a bowl. Add the oil, stir well, and work the oil into the dry ingredients with your fingertips until no lumps remain; the mixture will be very dry. In a separate bowl, whisk the milk and the egg white together, and add to the cornmeal mixture. Do not overmix.

Lightly oil a 1.5 litre ($2\frac{1}{2}$ pint) baking dish. Pour the corn-bread batter into the dish. Spoon the beef and vegetables into the centre of the batter, leaving a 3.5 cm ($1\frac{1}{2}$inch) border all round. Bake the mixture for 25 minutes. Remove the dish from the oven and let it stand for 5 minutes before serving.

Gingered Prawns on Black Beans

Serves 6

Working time: about 1 hour

Total time: about 9 hours

Calories 425
Protein 30g
Cholesterol 110mg
Total fat 6g
Saturated fat 1g
Sodium 345mg

600 g	large raw prawns, peeled and deveined, shells reserved	1¼ lb	4	garlic cloves, 2 crushed and 2 very thinly sliced	4
2.5 cm	piece of fresh ginger root, thinly sliced, plus 1 tbsp chopped fresh ginger root	1 inch	1	cinnamon stick, broken into 4 freshly ground black pepper	1
35 cl	dry white wine	12 fl oz	1 tbsp	grated lemon rind	1 tbsp
500 g	dried black beans, soaked for at least 8 hours and drained	1 lb	2 tbsp	virgin olive oil	2 tbsp
			¼ tsp	ground cinnamon	¼ tsp
¼ tsp	salt	¼ tsp	1 tsp	fresh lemon juice	1 tsp
2	onions, chopped	2	3	spring onions, trimmed and thinly sliced	3

Put the prawn shells in a large saucepan. Add the ginger slices, ¼ litre (8 fl oz) wine and ½ litre (16 fl oz) of water, and bring to the boil. Reduce the heat to medium and cook until reduced by half. Strain the stock into a bowl and set aside.

Meanwhile, put the drained beans in a large saucepan with the onions, crushed garlic, the pieces of cinnamon and some pepper. Cover well with water and boil for 10 minutes. Skim off the foam and reduce the heat to low. Add the stock, salt and lemon rind, and simmer until the beans are tender and

a thick sauce results. Remove cinnamon pieces.

About 5 minutes before the beans finish cooking, gently heat the oil in a large pan. Add the prawns and sprinkle with pepper. Add the chopped ginger, the thinly sliced garlic and the ground cinnamon, and sauté the prawns, stirring frequently, for 3 minutes. Pour the lemon juice and the remaining wine into the pan; continue cooking the mixture until the prawns are opaque and the liquid is reduced to a glaze. Stir in the spring onions.

Pour the beans onto a serving platter and top with the prawn mixture.

21

Seven-Spice Stew with Mussels, Squid and Prawns

Serves 6

Working
(and total)
time: about
1 hour

Calories
165
Protein
17g
Cholesterol
130mg
Total fat
2g
Saturated fat
0g
Sodium
265mg

750 g	mussels, scrubbed and debearded	1½ lb		1	whole garlic bulb, cloves peeled and thinly sliced	1
250 g	squid, cleaned and skinned	8 oz		¼ litre	dry white wine	8 fl oz
250 g	large raw prawns, peeled and deveined	8 oz		¼ tsp	each ground turmeric, cumin, coriander	¼ tsp
1	onion, chopped	1		⅛ tsp	each ground allspice, cloves, cardamom	⅛ tsp
2	ripe tomatoes, skinned, seeded and chopped	2		⅛ tsp	cayenne pepper	⅛ tsp

Put the mussels in a deep pan, together with the onion and the wine. Cover the pan tightly and cook the mussels over medium-high heat until they open. Discard any mussels that remain closed. Let the mussels cool, then remove them from their shells and set them aside. Strain the mussel-cooking liquid into a bowl and let it stand for 2 to 3 minutes to allow any sand to settle out. Slowly pour most of the liquid into a large, heavy-frying pan, leaving the sand behind.

Add the tomatoes, garlic and the spices to the frying pan. Bring the liquid to the boil, then reduce the heat to medium low and simmer the mixture until the garlic is tender.

Meanwhile, prepare the squid. Slit the pouches up one side and lay them flat on the work surface. Use a sharp knife to score a criss-cross pattern on the inside of each pouch. Cut the scored pouches into 4 cm (1½ inch) squares. Chop the tentacles into small pieces.

Add the squid to the liquid simmering in the frying pan. Cover the pan and cook until the squid pieces have curled up. Add the prawns, cover the pan and continue cooking until the prawns are opaque. Finally, add the mussels and cook the stew for 1 minute to heat the mussels through. Serve at once.

Grilled Prawns with Tomato-Ginger Sauce

Serves 4

Working time: about 40 minutes

Total time: about 1 hour and 15 minutes

Calories 215
Protein 17g
Cholesterol 130mg
Total fat 8g
Saturated fat 1g
Sodium 70mg

24	large raw prawns peeled and deveined	24
1	onion, chopped	1
12.5 cl	dry white wine	4 fl oz
2 tbsp	fresh lemon juice	2 tbsp
1 tbsp	virgin olive oil	1 tbsp
	Tomato-ginger sauce	
1 tbsp	virgin olive oil	1 tbsp
3	spring onions, trimmed and chopped	3
6	garlic cloves, chopped	6

1 tbsp	finely chopped fresh ginger root	1 tbsp
2	fresh green chili peppers, seeded and chopped	2
$\frac{1}{4}$ tsp	ground coriander	$\frac{1}{4}$ tsp
$\frac{1}{4}$ tsp	ground cumin	$\frac{1}{4}$ tsp
$\frac{1}{4}$ tsp	dry mustard	$\frac{1}{4}$ tsp
3	ripe tomatoes, skinned, seeded and chopped	
1 tsp	brown sugar	1 tsp
1 tbsp	red wine vinegar	1 tbsp

In a bowl, combine the onion, wine, lemon juice and oil. Add the prawns and let them marinate in the refrigerator for 1 hour.

Meanwhile, make the sauce. Pour the oil into a large, heavy frying pan over medium-high heat. When the oil is hot, add the spring onions, garlic, ginger and chili peppers; cook for 2 minutes, stirring constantly. Stir in the coriander, cumin and mustard, and cook the mixture for 1 minute more. Add the tomatoes and cook them, stirring constantly, for 1

minute. Remove the pan from the heat and stir in the brown sugar and vinegar. Transfer the sauce to a serving bowl and let it cool.

Near the end of the marinating time, preheat the grill. Thread the prawns in interlocking pairs on to four skewers. Brush the prawns with any remaining marinade and grill them about 5 cm (2 inches) below the heat source until they are opaque.

Serve the prawns on their skewers atop a bed of rice, with the sauce presented alongside.

Vegetable Stew, East Indian-Style

Serves 6

Working time: about 1 hour

Total time: about 2 hours

Calories 295
Protein 16g
Cholesterol 10mg
Total fat 13g
Saturated fat 3g
Sodium 330mg

1 tbsp	safflower oil	1 tbsp
15 g	unsalted butter	½ oz
1 tbsp	fresh ginger root, chopped	1 tbsp
1	medium onion, thinly sliced	1
2	bunches of spring onions, sliced	2
3	garlic cloves, thinly sliced	3
1 tsp	crushed saffron threads	1 tsp
½ tsp	each of ground cardamom cumin and cinnamon	½ tsp
¼ tsp	salt freshly ground black pepper	¼ tsp
2 litres	unsalted vegetable stock	3½ pints
2	potatoes, cut into small cubes	2
6	sticks celery, julienned	6
2	carrots, julienned	2

4 tsp	cornflour	4 tsp
150 g	spring greens, chopped	5 oz
150 g	stemmed kale, chopped	5 oz
125 g	stemmed spinach, chopped	4 oz
500 g	firm tofu (bean curd), cut into 2.5 cm (1 inch) cubes	1 lb
45 g	unsalted pistachios, chopped	½ oz
Cucumber-yogurt sauce		
4 tbsp	plain low-fat yogurt	4 tbsp
250 g	cucumber, peeled, chopped	8 oz
1	tomato, skinned, chopped	1
1 tbsp	chopped onion	1 tbsp
2 tbsp	chopped fresh coriander	2 tbsp
⅛ tsp	salt	⅛ tsp
¼ tsp	ground cumin	¼ tsp

To prepare the sauce, combine the yogurt, cucumber, tomato, onion, coriander, salt and cumin in a bowl then refrigerate it.

Fry the ginger in the oil for 1 minute. Add the onions and spring onions and cook for 5 minutes. Add the garlic, spices, salt and plenty of pepper; cook for 2 minutes.

Pour in all but 12.5 cl (4 fl oz) of the stock and add the potatoes. Simmer, covered, for 10 minutes. Add the celery and carrots, and cook until the potatoes are tender. Add the cornflour, blended with the remaining stock. Simmer to thicken.

Stir in the spring greens, kale and spinach, and simmer until they are tender. Add the tofu; pass the sauce and pistachios separately.

Seafood Chili with Peppers

Serves 4

Working time: about 1 hour and 30 minutes

Total time: about 3 hours and 30 minutes

Calories 450
Protein 34g
Cholesterol 70mg
Total fat 14g
Saturated fat 1g
Sodium 305mg

185 g	dried black beans, rinsed, soaked and cooked	**6½oz**	**1**	onion, cut into chunks	**1**
250 g	queen scallops, rinsed	**8 oz**	**½tsp**	dried tarragon	**½tsp**
125 g	prawns, peeled	**4 oz**	**¼tsp**	salt	**¼tsp**
125 g	haddock fillet, cut in pieces	**4 oz**	**¼tsp**	ground cloves	**¼tsp**
1	lime, sliced into thin rounds	**1**	**⅛tsp**	ground cinnamon	**⅛tsp**
1¼tsp	ground cumin	**1¼tsp**	**⅛tsp**	cayenne pepper	**⅛tsp**
⅛tsp	ground ginger	**⅛tsp**	**35 cl**	unsalted chicken stock	**12 fl oz**
3¼tsp	chili powder	**3¼tsp**	**400 g**	canned chopped tomatoes	**14 oz**
3 tbsp	fresh coriander, chopped	**3 tbsp**	**10**	small green tomatoes	**10**
2	garlic cloves, finely chopped	**2**	**1**	sweet red pepper, seeded, cut into chunks	**1**
½	green chili pepper, chopped	**½**	**1**	sweet yellow pepper, seeded cut into chunks	**1**
3 tbsp	safflower oil	**3 tbsp**			

Combine the scallops, prawns, fish pieces, lime, ¼ teaspoon of the cumin, the ginger, ¼ teaspoon of the chili powder, 1 tablespoon of the fresh coriander, half the garlic, the chili pepper and 1 tablespoon of the oil in a large bowl. Marinate for 30 minutes.

Meanwhile, heat the remaining oil and sauté the green tomatoes and peppers for 2 minutes. Add the onion and remaining garlic, and cook until the onion is translucent—about

5 minutes. Add the remaining spices and cook for 2 to 3 minutes. Add the stock and tomatoes, bring to the boil then cover and simmer until thickened. Add the beans and set aside.

With the remaining oil, sauté the green tomatoes and peppers for 2 minutes. Spread the cooked vegetables over the chili base and simmer. Lay the marinated seafood on top of the vegetables, cover, and steam until the fish is opaque. Serve with coriander garnish.

Plaice Curry

Serves 4

Working time: about 30 minutes

Total time: about 40 minutes

Calories 280
Protein 25g
Cholesterol 55mg
Total fat 7g
Saturated fat 1g
Sodium 205mg

1 tbsp	chopped fresh ginger root	1 tbsp	
½ tsp	turmeric	½ tsp	
¼ tsp	ground cumin	¼ tsp	
¼ tsp	ground coriander	¼ tsp	
⅛ tsp	ground cardamom	⅛ tsp	
⅛ tsp	fennel seeds	⅛ tsp	
⅛ tsp	ground mace	⅛ tsp	
½	lemon, juice only	½	
1 tbsp	safflower oil	1 tbsp	
2	onions, sliced	2	

750 g	ripe tomatoes, skinned, seeded and chopped, or 400 g (14 oz) canned tomatoes, drained and crushed	1½ lb
¼ litre	fish stock or unsalted chicken stock	16 fl oz
500 g	mushrooms, wiped clean and halved	1 lb
500 g	plaice fillets (or other white-fleshed fish)	1 lb

Put the ginger, turmeric, cumin, coriander, cardamom, fennel seeds and mace into a mortar; with a pestle, grind the seasonings to a paste. Set the paste aside.

Heat the oil in a large, non-reactive, heavy sauté pan over medium-high heat. Add the onions and sauté them until they are translucent—about 4 minutes. Stir in the spice paste, tomatoes and stock, and bring the liquid to the boil. Add the mushrooms and lemon juice. Lower the heat and simmer the curry until it is reduced by half—8 to 12 minutes.

Meanwhile, rinse the fillets under cold running water and pat them dry with paper towels. Slice the fillets into 2.5 cm (1 inch) wide strips. Lay the strips on top of the curry, cover the pan, and steam the fish until it is opaque—about 2 minutes. Serve immediately.

Prawn Creole

Serves 4

Working time: about 35 minutes

Total time: about 1 hour and 15 minutes

Calories 325
Protein 23g
Cholesterol 165mg
Total fat 6g
Saturated fat 1g
Sodium 240mg

4 tsp	safflower oil	4 tsp
1	large onion, thinly sliced	1
2	garlic cloves, finely chopped	2
1 tbsp	flour	1 tbsp
1 tbsp	chili powder	1 tbsp
600 g	large uncooked prawns, peeled, deveined if necessary, shells reserved	1¼ lb
¼ litre	dry white vermouth	8 fl oz

90 g	long-grain rice	3 oz
3	small sweet green peppers, seeded and cut into strips	3
1	stick celery, diagonally sliced	1
750 g	ripe tomatoes, skinned, seeded, chopped or 400g (14 oz) canned tomatoes, chopped	1½ lb
¼ tsp	filé powder (optional)	¼ tsp
¼ tsp	salt	¼ tsp

Heat 2 teaspoons of the oil in a saucepan over medium heat. Add the onion slices and cook them, stirring frequently, until they are browned—8 to 10 minutes. Remove half of the slices and set them aside.

Add the garlic and cook it for 1 minute. Stir in the flour and chili powder, then the prawn shells, vermouth and ¼ litre (8 fl oz) of water. Bring the liquid to a simmer; reduce the heat to medium low, cover the pan and cook the mixture for 20 minutes to make a flavourful base for the stew.

Meanwhile, bring ¼ litre (8 fl oz) of water to the boil in a small saucepan. Add the rice, stir once and reduce the heat to simmer; cook, covered, until the liquid is absorbed—about 20 minutes. Set aside.

Heat the remaining oil in a large, heavy frying pan over medium-high heat. Add the prawns and sauté them, stirring, for 2 minutes. Stir in the peppers and celery and cook for 1 minute. Add the tomatoes, the reserved onion slices and the filé powder if using. Strain the stew base into the frying pan and add the rice. Gently simmer for 5 minutes. Remove from heat and serve.

Southwest Gumbo

Serves 8

Working time:
about 40
minutes

Total time:
about 1 hour

Calories
290
Protein
32g
Cholesterol
110mg
Total fat
8g
Saturated fat
1g
Sodium
390mg

3 tbsp	olive oil	3 tbsp		1 litre	fishstock	1¾ pints
250 g	fresh okra, trimmed and cut into 2.5cm (1 inch) lengths	8 oz		1	sweet green pepper, chopped	1
				1	sweet red pepper, chopped	1
1	large onion, coarsely chopped	1		500 g	green tomatoes, cut into thin wedges	1 lb
120 g	celery, finely chopped	4 oz				
1	large garlic clove, finely chopped	1		6 tbsp	chopped fresh parsley	6 tbsp
1	large shallot, finely chopped	1		2 tbsp	chopped fresh coriander	2 tbsp
3 tbsp	masa harina	3 tbsp		8	drops Tabasco sauce	8
1 tsp	filé powder (optional)	1 tsp		500 g	halibut steaks, skinned, cut into 2.5 cm (1 inch) cubes	1 lb
1 tsp	salt	1 tsp				
1 tsp	sugar	1 tsp		500 g	monkfish fillet, cut into 2.5 cm (1 inch) pieces	1 lb
1 tsp	freshly ground black pepper	1 tsp				
1 tsp	ground cumin	1 tsp		500 g	prawns, peeled, deveined	1 lb

Sauté the okra in 1 tablespoon of the olive oil in a large pan over medium-high heat until it is evenly browned. Set aside when cooked.

Pour the remaining oil into the pan. Add the onion and celery and cook until the onion is translucent. Add the garlic and shallot and cook, stirring constantly, for 2 minutes more. Sprinkle in the masa harina, filé powder, salt, sugar, black pepper and cumin. Whisk in the stock and bring to the boil. Add the okra, green and red pepper, and the green tomatoes. Partially cover the pan, then reduce the heat to maintain a simmer and cook, stirring occasionally, for 8 to 10 minutes.

Stir in the parsley, coriander and Tabasco sauce. Add the halibut, monkfish and prawns, and gently stir the gumbo to incorporate the fish and prawns. Cover the pan, reduce the heat to low and cook the gumbo for 5 minutes more. Serve immediately.

Mexican Chicken Stew with Chilies

Serves 4

Working time: about 25 minutes

Total time: about 45 minutes

Calories 260
Protein 30g
Cholesterol 75mg
Total fat 11g
Saturated fat 2g
Sodium 680mg

1 litre	unsalted chicken stock	1¾ pints	1 tbsp	finely chopped garlic	1 tbsp
2	large dried mild chili peppers, seeded, rinsed and quartered	2	½ tsp	ground cumin	½ tsp
			⅛ tsp	ground cloves	⅛ tsp
500 g	boneless chicken breasts, skinned and cut into cubes	1 lb	350 g	chayote squash or young courgettes, cut into chunks	12 oz
1 tsp	salt	1 tsp	1	onion, coarsely chopped	1
¼ tsp	freshly ground black pepper	¼ tsp	2 tsp	cornflour, mixed with 2 tbsp water	2 tsp
1½ tbsp	corn or safflower oil	1½ tbsp	45 g	fresh coriander, chopped	1½ oz

Bring litre (8 fl oz) of the stock to the boil in a small saucepan. Add the chilies, then reduce the heat, cover the pan, and simmer for 5 minutes. Turn off the heat and let stand for 5 minutes. Purée the chilies in a blender with 4 tablespoons of the liquid. Blend in the remaining liquid and then set aside.

Toss the chicken cubes with the salt and pepper. Heat 1 tablespoon of oil in a large, heavy-bottomed sauté pan over medium-high heat. Add the cubes and sauté them, stirring frequently, until browned. Remove the cubes and set aside.

Reduce the heat to low; add the remaining oil, the garlic, cumin and cloves. Cook, stirring constantly, until the garlic has softened. Add the chili purée and the remaining stock.

Bring the liquid to the boil, then add the squash or courgettes and onion. Reduce the heat, cover the pan and simmer the mixture for 10 minutes. Remove the lid and increase the heat to medium; add the reserved chicken cubes, then stir in the cornflour mixture. Simmer the stew until it thickens slightly and is shiny. Stir in the coriander just before serving.

Java Lamb Curry with Tamarind

Serves 4

Working time: about 30 minutes

Total time: about 1 hour and 30 minutes

Calories 375
Protein 24g
Cholesterol 55mg
Total fat 24g
Saturated fat 13g
Sodium 380mg

500 g	lean lamb, cubed	1 lb	½ litre	unsalted brown stock	16 fl oz
1 tbsp	ground coriander	1 tbsp	75 g	tamarind pulp, steeped in	2½ oz
2 tsp	ground cumin	2 tsp		boiling water for 10 minutes, liquid	
¼ tsp	crushed hot red pepper	¼ tsp		strained and reserved	
	flakes or chili paste		6 tbsp	unsweetened coconut milk	6 tbsp
½ tsp	freshly ground black pepper	½ tsp	½ tsp	salt	½ tsp
1 tbsp	flour	1 tbsp	½ tsp	ground cinnamon	½ tsp
1 tbsp	safflower oil	1 tbsp	⅛ tsp	ground cloves	⅛ tsp
1	large onion, chopped	1	1	lemon, rind julienned,	1
1	sweet red pepper, chopped	1		juice reserved	
1 tbsp	fresh ginger root, chopped	1 tbsp	200 g	cauliflower florets	7 oz
2	garlic cloves, finely chopped	2	1	lemon (optional), sliced	1

Toss the lamb with the coriander, cumin, red pepper flakes, black pepper and flour. Heat the oil in a large, heavy-bottomed pan over medium-high heat. Add the lamb and sauté it, in several batches if necessary, until it is browned on all sides. Stir in the onion, red pepper, ginger and garlic. Reduce the heat to medium; cover the pan and cook the mixture, stirring frequently to keep the onions from burning, for 8 minutes.

Add the stock, tamarind liquid, coconut milk, salt, cinnamon and cloves. Bring the mixture to a simmer, then reduce the heat so that the liquid barely trembles; cover the pan and cook the mixture for 45 minutes. Stir in the lemon rind, lemon juice and cauliflower. Continue to simmer the curry, covered, until the cauliflower is tender. If you like, garnish the curry with the lemon slices before serving.

Chunky Beef Chili

Serves 8		
Working time: about 1 hour		
Total time: about 4 hours		

Calories 230	
Protein 27g	
Cholesterol 75mg	
Total fat 10g	
Saturated fat 3g	
Sodium 460mg	

2	large dried mild chili peppers, quartered	2	1 tbsp	ground cumin	1 tbsp
			1 tbsp	dried oregano	1 tbsp
2	hot green chili peppers seeded and chopped	2	$\frac{1}{4}$ tsp	cayenne pepper	$\frac{1}{4}$ tsp
			$\frac{1}{4}$ tsp	freshly ground black pepper	$\frac{1}{4}$ tsp
2 tbsp	safflower oil	2 tbsp	1 tbsp	plain flour	1 tbsp
1 kg	braising steak, cubed	2 lb	400 g	canned tomatoes, coarsely chopped with their juice	14 oz
2	large onions, finely chopped	2			
2	sticks celery, finely chopped	2	1	bay leaf	1
2	garlic cloves, finely chopped	2	$1\frac{1}{2}$ tsp	salt	$1\frac{1}{2}$ tsp
2 tbsp	fresh ginger root, chopped	2 tbsp	$\frac{1}{2}$ tsp	grated orange rind	$\frac{1}{2}$ tsp

Put the dried chillies into a small pan; pour in a litre (16 fl oz) of water and boil for 5 minutes. Turn off the heat and let the chillies soften for 5 minutes. Transfer to a blender with 12.5 cl (4 fl oz) soaking liquid; reserve remaining liquid. Add the fresh chilis and purée until very smooth. Strain through a sieve into the reserved soaking liquid.

Heat $\frac{1}{2}$ tablespoon oil in a large frying pan over medium-high heat. Add about one quarter of the beef and cook, turning frequently, until browned all over. Transfer to a large, heavy-bottomed pan. Brown the rest

of the meat the same way, using all but the tablespoon of the remaining oil.

Add the last of the oil to the frying pan with the onions, celery and garlic. Sauté for 5 minutes, stirring frequently. Stir in the ginger, cumin, oregano, cayenne pepper and black pepper, and cook for 1 minute. Add the flour and cook for 1 minute more, stirring constantly. Transfer the mixture to the pan.

Pour the reserved chili mixture and $\frac{1}{2}$ litre (16 fl oz) of water. Stir in the tomatoes with the bay leaf, salt and orange rind. Cook gently until meat is tender—$2\frac{1}{2}$ to 3 hours.

Boiled Yam with Hot Pepper Sauce

Serves 4

Working
(and total)
time: about
50 minutes

Calories
350
Protein
8g
Cholesterol
0mg
Total fat
4g
Saturated fat
0g
Sodium
245mg

1 tbsp	peanut oil	1 tbsp
2	large onions, chopped	2
750 g	tomatoes, skinned and seeded chopped	1½ lb
1	hot yellow chili pepper, or one hot red chili pepper, chopped	1

3 tbsp	tomato paste	3 tbsp
½ tsp	salt	½ tsp
1 tsp	vegetable extract	1 tsp
1 kg	firm yam, peeled	2 lb
1 tbsp	finely chopped parsley, for garnish	1 tbsp

In a heavy-bottomed saucepan, heat the oil over medium heat. Add the onions and cook them, stirring frequently, until they are golden—about 5 minutes. Add the tomatoes and chili pepper to the pan and stir them briskly for about 8 minutes, to cook them through. Stir in the tomato paste and 4 tablespoons of cold water then add the salt and the vegetable extract. Mix the ingredients in the pan thoroughly. Reduce the heat, cover the pan, and simmer the sauce for 10 minutes. Set the sauce aside and keep it warm.

Rinse the yam under cold running water and cut it into thin slices about 1 cm (½ inch) thick. Place the slices in a large saucepan of water; the water should just cover the yam. Bring the water to the boil, reduce the heat to medium and cook the yam slices, with the pan partially covered, for 3 to 4 minutes, or until they feel soft when pierced with a sharp knife; be careful not to overcook them. Drain the slices in a colander.

Serve the yam slices with the hot pepper sauce, garnished with the chopped parsley.

Spiced Red Cabbage

Serves 6	
Working time: about 20 minutes	
Total time: about 1 hour 50 minutes	

Calories 330	
Protein 15g	
Cholesterol 20mg	
Total fat 13g	
Saturated fat 4g	
Sodium 390mg	

1 tbsp	juniper berries	**1 tbsp**
1 tbsp	coriander seeds	**1 tbsp**
2 tbsp	virgin olive oil	**2 tbsp**
5	garlic cloves, sliced	**5**
1	large red cabbage, sliced	**1**
30 cl	dry cider	**½ pint**

	freshly ground black pepper	
3	large green cooking apples cored, peeled, halved and placed in acidulated water	**3**
90 g	matured Edam cheese, thinly sliced	**3 oz**

Preheat the oven to 180°C (350°F or Mark 4). Crush the juniper berries and coriander seeds using a mortar and pestle.

Heat the oil over medium heat in a 7 litre (12 pint) fireproof casserole. Add the garlic and crushed spices and stir-fry them briefly, then add the red cabbage and stir-fry for 3 to 4 minutes. Remove the casserole from the heat. Pour the cider over the cabbage and season it with black pepper. Cover the casserole and cook the cabbage in the oven for 1 hour.

Stir the cabbage and transfer it to a 3.5 litre

(6 pint) ovenproof casserole—the cabbage will have halved in volume by this stage. Drain the apple halves, pat them dry on paper towels and lay them on top of the cabbage. Cover the casserole and return cabbage to the oven for a further 30 minutes.

Preheat the grill to medium. Remove the casserole from the oven, take off the lid and, without stirring the contents, lay the slices of cheese over the apples. Put the casserole under the grill for about 5 minutes, until the cheese has melted and begun to brown. Serve the cabbage at once.

Chestnut-Stuffed Sweet Potatoes with Chili Sauce

Serves 4

Working time:
about 1 hour
10 minutes

Total time:
about 2 hours

Calories
455
Protein
6g
Cholesterol
0mg
Total fat
11g
Saturated fat
2g
Sodium
165mg

2	large sweet potatoes, scrubbed	2
400 g	fresh chestnuts, peeled	4 oz
1 tbsp	virgin olive oil	1 tbsp
1	onion, finely chopped	1
1	garlic clove, crushed	1
$\frac{1}{4}$ tsp	salt	$\frac{1}{4}$ tsp
$\frac{1}{2}$	lime, juice only	$\frac{1}{2}$
1	bunch watercress, stemmed	1
$\frac{1}{2}$	orange, rind julienned, blanched for 1 minute and drained, flesh segmented	$\frac{1}{2}$

Chili sauce		
1 tbsp	virgin olive oil	1 tbsp
$\frac{1}{2}$	onion, finely chopped	$\frac{1}{2}$
1	garlic clove, crushed	1
$\frac{1}{2}$	red chili pepper, fresh or dried, finely chopped	$\frac{1}{2}$
$\frac{1}{2}$ tsp	ground cumin	$\frac{1}{2}$ tsp
175 g	tomatoes, skinned and seeded chopped	6 oz
2 tsp	demerara sugar	2 tsp
1 tsp	red wine vinegar	1 tsp

Preheat the oven to 200°C (400°F or Mark 6).

Prick the sweet potatoes and bake them on a rack in the oven for about $1\frac{1}{2}$ hours, or until tender when pierced.

For the chili sauce, heat the oil in a pan and fry the onion, garlic and chili until soft. Stir in the cumin, cover and cook gently for a further 4 minutes. Mix in the tomatoes, sugar and vinegar and simmer, covered, for 10 minutes. Let the sauce cool a little, then blend it in a food processor or blender until smooth.

Simmer the peeled chestnuts in boiling water for until soft. Drain and chop. Heat the oil in a saucepan, add the onion and garlic, and cook until soft. Add the chestnuts, with the salt and lime juice. Keep the stuffing warm.

Cut the potatoes in half lengthwise and scoop out the flesh. Mash and spoon it back into the shells, making a well in the centre. Pile in the chestnut stuffing. Reheat the sauce, then transfer it to a bowl. Arrange the potatoes on a bed of watercress and garnish with the orange segments and rind.

Potato, Carrot and Cauliflower Curry

Serves 6

Working time: about 30 minutes

Total time: about 1 hour

Calories 230
Protein 6g
Cholesterol 0mg
Total fat 11g
Saturated fat 5g
Sodium 230mg

2 tbsp	virgin olive oil	2 tbsp
2	onions, finely chopped	2
60 g	fresh ginger root, grated	2 oz
3	garlic cloves, crushed	3
2	fresh hot green chili peppers, seeded and finely chopped	2
2 tsp	paprika	2 tsp
½ tsp	ground tumeric	½ tsp
1 tsp	ground cumin	1 tsp
45 cl	unsalted vegetable stock	¼ pint
500 g	potatoes, cut into dice	1 lb
250 g	carrots, cut into dice	8 oz
250 g	cauliflower florets	8 oz
175 g	French beans, trimmed and cut into 2.5 cm (1 inch) lengths	6 oz
175 g	garden peas	6 oz
90 g	coconut milk powder or creamed coconut	3 oz
1 tbsp	cornflour, blended with 3 tbsp cold water	1 tbsp
½ tsp	salt	½ tsp
	freshly ground black pepper	

Put the olive oil and onions into a large bowl. Microwave on high, uncovered, for 5 to 6 minutes, until the onions are softened, stirring half way through the cooking time. Stir in the ginger, garlic, chillies, paprika, turmeric and cumin and cook on high, uncovered, for 2 minutes. Add the stock, potatoes, carrots and cauliflower and stir well, then cover the bowl with plastic film, pulling back one corner to allow steam to escape. Cook on high for 20 minutes, stirring every 5 minutes. Then stir in the beans and peas and cook, covered as before, for a further 10 minutes, until the vegetables are tender.

Stir the coconut milk and cornflour mixtures into the vegetables and cook, uncovered, on high for 5 minutes, stirring half way through. Season with the salt and some black pepper. Allow the curry to stand for 5 minutes before serving.

Saffron and Potato Stew with Rouille

Serves 6

Working time:
about 40
minutes

Total time:
about 55
minutes

Calories
270
Protein
7g
Cholesterol
0mg
Total fat
3g
Saturated fat
trace
Sodium
350mg

750 g	potatoes, cut into chunks	1½ lb		30 cl	medium white wine	½ pint
1 tsp	virgin olive oil	1 tsp		90 g	small pasta shapes	3 oz
2	beef tomatoes, skinned and seeded, cut into chunks	2		250 g	courgettes, sliced	8 oz
				3 tbsp	chopped parsley	3 tbsp
2	leeks, white and green parts separated and sliced	2		1	yellow pepper, sliced	1
					freshly ground black pepper	
1	onion sliced	1		45 g	thick Greek yogurt	1½ oz
2 tsp	chopped fresh thyme	2 tsp			**Rouille**	
3	bay leaves	3		60 g	white breadcrumbs	2 oz
1 tsp	caster sugar	1 tsp		8 cl	skimmed milk	3 fl oz
2	strips thinly pared orange rind	2		2	hot red chili peppers, chopped	2
1 tsp	saffron, soaked in 1 tbsp boiling water	1 tsp		3	garlic cloves, roughly chopped	3
				¼ tsp	salt	¼ tsp
60 cl	unsalted vegetable stock	1 pint		1	small red pepper, chopped	1

Steep the breadcrumbs in the milk for five minutes until soft. Purée the chili peppers, garlic, salt and sweet red pepper with 2 tablespoons of water. Add the bread and milk, and blend until smooth.

Boil the potatoes for 10 minutes, then drain.

Gently heat the oil in a large pan. Add the tomatoes, leeks, onion, herbs, and cook, stirring, for 5 minutes. Stir in the sugar,

orange rind, saffron, stock and wine, and bring to the boil. Add the pasta and cook, covered, for 5 to 7 minutes.

Stir in the remaining vegetables, salt and some black pepper and cook, stirring, until the potatoes are heated through but the courgettes still retain their crispness.

Serve individually with a swirl of yogurt and a spoonful of rouille on each portion.

Spiced Steak Phyllo Boats

Makes 30 boats

Working (and total) time: about 50 minutes

Per boat:
Calories 40
Protein 3g
Cholesterol 10mg
Total fat 2g
Saturated fat 1g
Sodium 10mg

6	sheets phyllo pastry, each about 45 by 30 cm (18 by 12 inches)	6
1½ tbsp	virgin olive oil	1½ tbsp
1	small onion, finely chopped	1
30 g	pine-nuts	1 oz
2	garlic cloves, crushed	2
1 tsp	ground cumin	1 tsp
1 tsp	ground cardamom	1 tsp
⅛ tsp	cayenne pepper	⅛ tsp
½ tsp	ground cinnamon	½ tsp
125 g	mushrooms, fincly chopped	4 oz
45 g	raisins, chopped	1½ oz
250 g	rumpsteak, minced	8 oz
¼ tsp	salt	¼ tsp
	freshly ground black pepper	
1 tbsp	finely cut chives	1 tbsp

Preheat the oven to 220°C (425°F or Mark 7).

Lay out three sheets of phyllo pastry, one on top of another. Using an inverted 11 by 5 cm (4½ by 2 inch) boat-shaped tartlet tin as a guide, cut out oval shapes. Fit the ovals into 9 by 4 cm (3½ by 1½ inch) boat-shaped tins. Trim with scissors. Repeat with the remaining phyllo sheets to fill 30 tartlet tins. Place on baking sheets and bake until the pastry is golden-brown—6 to 8 minutes. Remove the boats from the tins and cool on wire racks.

Heat half the oil in a heavy frying pan. Add the onion and cook gently until it is softened.

Add the pine-nuts, garlic, and spices. Cook for 2 to 3 minutes, then add the mushrooms and cook until they are softened and most of the liquid has evaporated—6 to 8 minutes. Stir in the raisins and set aside.

Heat the remaining oil in the frying pan until it begins to smoke. Add the steak and stir-fry it just long enough for the meat to change colour—do not overcook. Return the mushroom mixture to the pan and heat through. Season with salt and pepper.

Spoon the filling into the phyllo boats and sprinkle with the chives. Serve warm.

Spiced Peanut Dip with Crudité Skewers

Serves 10

Working time: about 1 hour and 30 minutes

Total time: about 5 hours

Calories 105
Protein 5g
Cholesterol 2mg
Total fat 6g
Saturated fat 1g
Sodium 165mg

15 cl	unsalted chicken stock	¼ pint
1 tsp	saffron threads	1 tsp
125 g	shelled peanuts	4 oz
1 tbsp	virgin olive oil	1 tbsp
1	large onion, very finely chopped	1
4	garlic cloves, crushed	4
30 g	fresh ginger root, sliced	1 oz
2 tsp	ground coriander	2 tsp
1 tsp	ground cumin	1 tsp

1 tsp	ground cardamom	1 tsp
30 cl	plain low-fat yogurt	½ pint
½ tsp	salt	½ tsp
	freshly ground black pepper	
2 tsp	finely cut fresh chives	2 tsp
1 tsp	finely chopped parsley	1 tsp
Crudité skewers		
1.25 kg	a selection of sweet peppers, celery, radishes, carrots	2½ lb

Preheat the oven to 220°C (425°F or Mark 7). In a saucepan, heat the chicken stock to boiling point; remove from the heat and add the saffron threads. Stir well and leave to stand for about 30 minutes.

Roast the peanuts on a baking sheet until their skins loosen. Rub in a clean tea towel to remove their skins. Heat the oil and cook until they are very soft but not browned. Stir in the garlic.

Put the ginger, coriander, cumin, cardamom, yogurt, peanuts and saffron mixture into a blender, and blend until smooth. Pour on to the onions and stir well. Cook over low heat until the mixture thickens—about 20 minutes. Season with the salt and some pepper. Pour into a bowl; cover closely with plastic film to prevent a skin forming. When cool, chill in the refrigerator for 3 to 4 hours, or overnight.

Just before serving, prepare the vegetables. Cut them into decorative shapes and thread them on to cocktail sticks. Stir the dip and spoon it into a serving bowl, then sprinkle the top with the chives and parsley. Place the bowl on a large serving platter and surround with the crudité skewers.

Sweet and Spicy Sweetcorn Salad

Serves 12
as a side
dish

Working
time: about
20 minutes

Total time:
about 25
minutes

Calories
105
Protein
2g
Cholesterol
0mg
Total fat
3g
Saturated fat
0g
Sodium
60mg

825 g	sweetcorn kernels (cut from 5 large ears)	1¾ lb	1	small red onion, chopped	1	
1	sweet red pepper, seeded, cut into thin, long strips	1	4 tbsp	red wine vinegar	4 tbsp	
1	sweet green pepper, seeded, cut into thin strips	1	1 tbsp	brown sugar	1 tbsp	
	small green chili peppers, seeded finely chopped	2	2 tbsp	safflower oil	2 tbsp	
			2 tsp	chopped fresh oregano, or ½ tsp dried oregano	2 tsp	
			¼ tsp	salt freshly ground black pepper	¼ tsp	

Fill a saucepan with about 2.5 cm (1 inch) water. Set a vegetable steamer in the pan and bring the water to the boil. Put the fresh sweetcorn into the steamer, cover the pan, and steam the sweetcorn until it is just tender—about 3 minutes.

In a large bowl, combine the wine vinegar, sugar, oil, oregano, salt and pepper. Add the sweetcorn, the peppers and the onion, and toss the mixture well. Serve the salad at room temperature, or refrigerate it for at least 1 hour and serve it well chilled.

Curried Cabbage Coleslaw

Serves 6 as a side dish	
Working time: about 20 minutes	
Total time: about 1 hour and 20 minutes	

Calories 60	
Protein 2g	
Cholesterol 4mg	
Total fat 2g	
Saturated fat 1g	
Sodium 145mg	

15 cl	soured cream	5 fl oz			freshly ground black pepper	
2 tsp	curry powder	2 tsp	500 g	white cabbage, finely shredded	1 lb
2 tsp	tomato paste	2 tsp	1	red apple, quartered,	1
2 tsp	lemon juice	2 tsp	40 g	raisins	1½ oz
½ tsp	salt	½ tsp	1 tbsp	chopped fresh coriander	1 tbsp

Put the soured cream, curry powder, tomato paste, lemon juice, salt and some freshly ground pepper into a large bowl and stir well. Add the shredded cabbage, sliced apple and the raisins and mix well together. Cover the bowl, then set it aside in a cool place for at least 1 hour to allow the flavours to mellow.

Just before serving, spoon the salad into a serving bowl and garnish with the coriander.

Curried Black-Eyed Peas

Serves 6 as
a side dish

Working
time: about
20 minutes

Total time:
about 2
hours and
30 minutes

Calories
105

Protein
5g

Cholesterol
0mg

Total fat
3g

Saturated fat
0g

Sodium
100mg

170 g	black-eyed peas picked over	6 oz
	picked over	
¼ tsp	salt	¼ tsp
12.5 cl	unsalted chicken stock	4 fl oz
2	bunches spring onions,	2
	cut in 2.5 cm (1 inch) lengths	
1½ tbsp	fresh lemon juice	1½ tbsp

1 tbsp	red or white wine vinegar	1 tbsp
½ tbsp	honey	½ tbsp
1¼ tsp	curry powder	1¼ tsp
	freshly ground black pepper	
1 tbsp	virgin olive oil	1 tbsp
½	sweet red pepper, seeded,	½
	and cut into bâtonnets	

Rinse the black-eyed peas, then put them into a large saucepan, and pour in enough cold water to cover them Discard any peas that float to the surface. Bring the water to the boil and cook the peas for 2 minutes. Turn off the heat, partially cover the pan, and soak the peas for at least 1 hour. (Alternatively, soak the peas overnight in cold water.)

Simmer the peas over medium-low heat and tightly cover the pan. Cook, occasionally skimming any foam from the surface of the liquid, until they begin to soften—about 45 minutes. Stir in the salt and continue cooking until tender. If the peas appear to be drying out at any point, pour in a little more water.

Meanwhile, heat the stock in a large frying pan over medium heat. Add the spring onions and partially cover the pan. Cook, stirring often, until almost all the liquid has evaporated—8 to 10 minutes. Transfer to a bowl.

In a smaller bowl, combine the lemon juice, vinegar, honey, curry powder and some pepper. Whisk in the oil and set aside.

Transfer the cooked peas to a colander; rinse and drain them. Add the peas and the red pepper to the spring onions in the bowl. Pour the dressing over all and toss the salad well. Chill the salad before serving.

Black Bean, Rice and Pepper Salad

<table>
<tr><td>Serves 4 as a main course</td></tr>
<tr><td>Working time: about 20 minutes</td></tr>
<tr><td>Total time: about 11 hours</td></tr>
</table>

<table>
<tr><td>Calories 635</td></tr>
<tr><td>Protein 21g</td></tr>
<tr><td>Cholesterol 2mg</td></tr>
<tr><td>Total fat 10g</td></tr>
<tr><td>Saturated fat 1g</td></tr>
<tr><td>Sodium 385mg</td></tr>
</table>

185 g	black beans, picked over, soaked for 8 hours, drained	**6½ oz**
1	small onion, chopped	**1**
1	garlic clove	**1**
2 tsp	fresh thyme, or ½ tsp dried thyme leaves	**2 tsp**
1	bay leaf	**1**
½ tsp	salt	**½ tsp**
1 litre	unsalted chicken stock	**1¼ pints**
370 g	long-grain rice	**13 oz**
2	shallots, finely chopped	**2**
1	green chili pepper, chopped	**1**
1	sweet red pepper, seeded, and sliced into short strips	**1**

1	sweet green pepper, seeded, and sliced into short strips	**1**
3	spring onions, trimmed and thinly sliced	**3**
2 tbsp	chopped fresh coriander	**2 tbsp**
	Chili dressing	
1 tsp	Dijon mustard	**1 tsp**
1 tbsp	sherry vinegar	**1 tbsp**
1 tbsp	unsalted chicken stock	**1 tbsp**
2 tbsp	virgin olive oil	**2 tbsp**
½ tsp	chili powder	**½ tsp**
4	drops Tabasco sauce	**4**
1	garlic clove, finely chopped freshly ground black pepper	**1**

Boil the beans, well-covered with water for 10 minutes, then drain. Return them to the pan, cover with water and boil. Add the onion, garlic, thyme and bay leaves, cover and simmer, skimming off any foam, until the beans are soft. Add salt and cook a little longer. Remove the garlic and bay leaf and drain and rinse the beans.

Bring the stock to the boil in a small saucepan. Add the rice and shallots, and lower the heat to maintain a simmer. Cook the rice, covered, until it is tender and the liquid is absorbed. While the rice cooks, whisk together the dressing ingredients.

Transfer the hot rice to a bowl. Add the peppers, spring onions and beans. Pour on the dressing, toss well, and chill for 1 hour. Sprinkle with fresh coriander before serving.

Saffron Chicken with Yogurt

Serves 6

Working time: about 30 minutes

Total time: about 1 day

Calories 210

Protein 28g

Cholesterol 90mg

Total fat 9g

Saturated fat 2g

Sodium 185mg

6	whole chicken legs, skinned	6	90 g	onion, chopped	3 oz
4 tbsp	unsalted chicken stock	4 tbsp	2	garlic cloves, finely chopped	2
⅛ tsp	saffron (about 20 threads)	⅛ tsp	1 tsp	grated fresh ginger root	1 tsp
¼ tsp	salt	¼ tsp	4 tbsp	fresh lemon juice	4 tbsp
	freshly ground black pepper		⅛ tsp	cayenne pepper	⅛ tsp
12.5 cl	plain low-fat yogurt	4 fl oz	¼ tsp	ground cumin	¼ tsp

Combine the stock and saffron in a small saucepan over medium heat and bring them to a simmer. Remove the pan from the heat and let the saffron steep for about 5 minutes The stock will turn golden.

Sprinkle the chicken legs with the salt and pepper. Put them in a shallow baking dish and dribble the stock and saffron mixture over them. Turn the legs to coat both sides and arrange them so that they do not touch.

Combine the, yogurt, onion, garlic, ginger, lemon juice, cayenne pepper and cumin in a food processor or blender, and purée until smooth. Pour the mixture over the chicken legs and cover the dish with a sheet of plastic film. Refrigerate it for 8 hours or overnight.

Preheat the grill. Remove the legs from the marinade and arrange them top side down in a foil-lined grill pan. Reserve the marinade. Position the grill pan 8 to 10 cm (3½ to 4 inches) below the heat source. Grill the chicken for about 8 minutes on each side, basting them with the marinade every 2 minutes. When the juices run clear from a thigh pierced with the tip of a sharp knife then the chicken is cooked.

Roast Gingered Turkey Breast

Serves 6		
Working time: about 10 minutes		
Total time: about 1 day		

Calories 160		
Protein 26g		
Cholesterol 60mg		
Total fat 5g		
Saturated fat 1g		
Sodium 165mg		

750 g	turkey breast, skinned and boned	**1½ lb**	**2 tbsp**	peeled and grated fresh ginger root	**2 tbsp**
2 tsp	safflower oil	**2 tsp**	**4 tbsp**	unsalted turkey or chicken stock	**4 tbsp**
	Ginger marinade		**1 tsp**	dark sesame oil	**1 tsp**
3	garlic cloves, finely chopped	**3**	**1 tbsp**	soy sauce	**1 tbsp**
¾ tsp	ground cinnamon	**¾ tsp**			

To make the marinade, combine the garlic, cinnamon, ginger, stock, sesame oil and soy sauce in a shallow bowl just large enough to hold the turkey breast. Using a knife with a sharp point, poke several deep slits in the thick part of the meat to allow the marinade to penetrate. Put the turkey in the bowl with the marinade and turn it to coat it. Cover the bowl and refrigerate for 8 to 24 hours, turning occasionally.

Preheat the oven to 180°C (350°F or Mark 4). Remove the turkey from the marinade, scraping any clinging garlic and ginger back into the bowl. Reserve the marinade and allow the turkey to come to room temperature. Heat the safflower oil in a shallow fireproof casserole over medium-high heat. Sauté the turkey until golden on one side and turn. Use a pastry brush to baste with the accumulated juices and continue cooking for 1 minute. Put the casserole in the oven and roast the turkey until it feels firm but springy to the touch basting once with the reserved marinade. Let the turkey rest for at least 5 minutes before slicing. Serve hot or cold.

Turkey Satays with Peanut Sauce

Serves 8

Working time:
about 30
minutes

Total time:
about 6 hours
and 15
minutes

Calories
235
Protein
29g
Cholesterol
60mg
Total fat
10g
Saturated fat
2g
Sodium
285mg

1 kg	turkey breast meat, skinned and cut into cubes	2 lb		2 tsp	paprika	2 tsp
	Marinade				**Peanut sauce**	
¼ litre	plain low-fat yogurt	8 fl oz		90 g	peanut butter	3 oz
4 tbsp	safflower oil	4 tbsp		¼ litre	boiling water	8 fl oz
1 tbsp	grated fresh ginger root	1 tbsp		2	garlic cloves, finely chopped	2
½ tsp	ground cardamom and ground coriander	½ tsp		2 tbsp	fresh lemon juice	2 tbsp
¼ tsp	salt	¼ tsp		2 tbsp	low-sodium soy sauce, or naturally fermented shoyu	2 tbsp
½ tsp	freshly ground black pepper	½ tsp		¼ tsp	crushed red pepper flakes	¼ tsp
				2 tbsp	molasses	2 tbsp

Whisk the marinade ingredients together. Add the cubed turkey and refrigerate for 6 hours or overnight, stirring occasionally to keep the pieces well coated.

Preheat the grill with its rack and pan in place about 10 minutes beforehand.

To make the peanut sauce, first heat the peanut butter in a saucepan over low heat. Whisk in the boiling water, then stir in the garlic, lemon juice, soy sauce, red pepper and molasses. Bring the mixture to the boil and

whisk it until it thickens. Pour into a sauceboat.

Thread the turkey cubes onto skewers, preferably square or flat-bladed, so the cubes will not slip when turned and cook unevenly. Grill the cubes, turning them several times, for about 10 to 15 minutes. To test for doneness, make a small cut in a turkey cube to see whether its centre has turned from pink to white. Arrange the satays on a heated platter and serve the sauce separately.

Turkey Curry with Puréed Yams

Serves 6

Working time: about 30 minutes

Total time: about 1 hour 45 minutes

Calories 335
Protein 25g
Cholesterol 75 mg
Total fat 12g
Saturated fat 6g
Sodium 255mg

600 g	boneless dark turkey meat, skinned and cubed	1¼ lb
45 g	unsalted butter	1½ oz
2	small yams or sweet potatoes, peeled and cubed	2
¾ litre	unsalted turkey or chicken stock	1¼ pints
2	medium onions, chopped	2
1	stick celery, chopped	1
2	garlic cloves. chopped	2

½ tsp	grated fresh ginger root, or ¼ tsp ground ginger	½ tsp
½ tsp	fresh thyme, or ⅛ tsp dried thyme	½ tsp
2 tbsp	curry powder	2 tbsp
5 tbsp	fresh lemon juice	5 tbsp
¼ tsp	salt	¼ tsp
	freshly ground black pepper	
60 g	sultanas	2 oz
150 g	peas	5 oz

In a saucepan, bring 1 litre (1¾ pints) of water to the boil. Add the turkey, blanch for 1 minute, and drain.

In a large, heavy frying pan over low heat, melt half of the butter. Add the yams and cook them slowly, stirring frequently, until they are browned and tender—about 25 minutes. Purée the yams with ¼ litre (8 fl oz) of stock in a food processor or blender, and set them aside.

Melt the remaining butter in the frying pan. Add the onions, celery, garlic, ginger and thyme. Cook, stirring frequently, until the onions begin to brown—about 15 minutes.

Add the turkey, curry powder, lemon juice, salt and pepper. Reduce the heat to low and gently stir in the rest of the stock. Cover and simmer for 45 minutes. Uncover the frying pan and add the sultanas and the yam purée. Cover the pan again and cook, stirring occasionally, until the turkey cubes are tender—about 30 minutes more. Add the peas and cook another 5 minutes. Serve the curry immediately.

Turkey and Green Chili Enchiladas

Serves 4

Working time:
about 40
minutes

Total time:
about 1 hour

Calories
455
Protein
38g
Cholesterol
70mg
Total fat
16g
Saturated fat
4g
Sodium
375mg

350 g	cooked turkey meat, chopped	12 oz	$\frac{1}{8}$ tbsp	sugar	$\frac{1}{8}$ tbsp
2 to 5	fresh green chili peppers, seeded, chopped	2 to 5	350 g	tomatillos, blanched, cored and quartered	12 oz
1	large onion, chopped	1	90 g	mild Cheddar cheese, grated	3 oz
1	large tomato, cored, seeded and chopped	1	$\frac{1}{2}$ tsp	ground cumin	$\frac{1}{2}$ tsp
			1 tsp	chopped fresh oregano	1 tsp
2	garlic cloves, chopped	2	$\frac{1}{8}$ tsp	salt	$\frac{1}{8}$ tsp
2 tbsp	chopped fresh coriander	2 tbsp	8	corn tortillas	8
4 tbsp	unsalted chicken stock	4 tbsp	12.5 cl	soured cream	4 fl oz
2 tbsp	fresh lemon juice	2 tbsp	12.5 cl	plain low-fat yogurt	4 fl oz

Preheat the oven to 180°C (350°F or Mark 4). Scrape three quarters of the chilies into a blender. Add the onion, tomato, garlic, coriander, stock, lemon juice and sugar. Using short bursts, process the mixture into a rough purée. Add the tomatillos and process until coarsely chopped. Pour into a saucepan and simmer it over medium heat for 10 minutes.

For the filling, combine the turkey, 60 g (2 oz) of the cheese, the remaining chilies, cumin, oregano, salt and half of the sauce.

Warm each tortilla in turn for 10 seconds in a heavy frying pan over medium heat. Place in the hot sauce, carefully turn over, and transfer it to a plate. Spoon some of the turkey filling down the centre of the tortilla, then roll it up to enclose the filling, and place seam side down in a large oiled baking dish.

Pour the rest of the hot sauce over the enchiladas and sprinkle them with the remaining cheese. Bake, uncovered, for 20 minutes. Meanwhile, combine the soured cream and yogurt as a topping; spoon it over the enchiladas just before serving.

Chopped Turkey with Lime and Coriander

Serves 26 to
32 as a party
snack, 8 as
a main
course

Working
(and Total)
time: about
30 minutes

Calories
160
Protein
16g
Cholesterol
30mg
Total fat
6g
Saturated fat
1g
Sodium
200mg

	Yogurt sauce				
½ litre	plain low-fat yogurt	8 fl oz	30 g	fresh breadcrumbs	1 oz
1 tsp	finely chopped fresh coriander	1 tsp	1	lime, rind only, grated	1
1 tsp	sugar	1 tsp	5 tbsp	finely sliced spring onion greens	5 tbsp
2 tbsp	fresh lime juice	2 tbsp	2 tsp	finely chopped fresh coriander	2 tsp
⅛ tsp	salt	⅛ tsp	¼ tsp	chili powder	¼ tsp
⅛ tsp	cayenne pepper	⅛ tsp	¼ tsp	salt	¼ tsp
	Turkey morsels		1	egg white	1
350 g	cooked turkey breast meat, finely chopped	12 oz	4 tbsp	plain flour	4 tbsp
			2 tbsp	safflower oil	2 tbsp

To prepare the sauce, pour the yogurt into a small bowl and whisk in the coriander, sugar, lime juice, salt and cayenne. Let stand 15 minutes.

Place the turkey in a bowl with the breadcrumbs, rind, spring onions, coriander, chili powder and salt. Add the egg white and knead by hand or mix with a spoon.

With dampened hands, gently form the meat mixture into balls the size of large marbles and lightly dust with flour. Heat the oil in a heavy frying pan over medium heat and fry as many balls as possible without crowding until brown all over—5 to 6 minutes. Transfer them to a warm platter and serve with the sauce.

Chicken and Mango Brochettes with Honey-Lime Sauce

Serves 8

Working time:
about 1 hour

Total time:
about 2 hours
and 30
minutes

Calories
110
Protein
15g
Cholesterol
40mg
Total fat
2g
Saturated fat
1g
Sodium
110mg

500 g	chicken breast fillets, skinned, cubed	1 lb	½ tsp	ground cardamom	½ tsp
2	firm ripe mangoes	2	½ tsp	ground cumin	½ tsp
1	lime, thinly sliced	1	½ tsp	ground coriander	½ tsp
	Spicy marinade		1 tsp	ground turmeric	1 tsp
1	small onion, chopped	1	2	garlic cloves, crushed	2
5 cm	piece fresh ginger root, very finely chopped	2 inch	¼ tsp	salt	¼ tsp
				Honey-lime sauce	
15 cl	plain low-fat yogurt	¼ pint	4 tbsp	clear honey	4 tbsp
			2	limes, finely grated rind and juice	2

Put all the ingredients for the marinade into a bowl and mix well. Add the chicken breasts, turning them until they are well coated with the marinade. Cover and allow to marinate at room temperature for 2 hours.

About 30 minutes before you are ready to serve the brochettes, prepare the sauce. Put the honey into a small saucepan with the lime rind and juice. Bring the mixture to the boil, reduce the heat and simmer gently until the sauce turns syrupy—about 20 minutes.

While the sauce simmers, skin the mangoes and cut the flesh away from the stones with a sharp knife. Cut the flesh into neat 2.5 cm (1 inch) cubes. Thread the marinated chicken and the mango on to eight skewers, alternating chicken cubes with pieces of fruit. Preheat the grill to high.

Place the brochettes on a rack and grill them until the chicken is cooked through—about 2 minutes on each side. The chicken needs only brief grilling; if it is overcooked, its lean flesh will quickly dry out.

To serve the brochettes, pour the lime sauce over them, and garnish them with the lime slices.

Devilled Mushroom Tartlets

Serves 8

Working time:
about 50
minutes

Total time:
about 1 hour
and 20
minutes

Calories
225
Protein
5g
Cholesterol
40mg
Total fat
15g
Saturated fat
5g
Sodium
130mg

600 g	small button mushrooms, trimmed and wiped clean	**1¼ lb**
1 tbsp	fresh lemon juice	**1 tbsp**
¼ tsp	salt	**¼ tsp**
	freshly ground black pepper	
15 cl	soured cream	**¼ pint**
1 tsp	prepared English mustard	**1 tsp**
⅛ tsp	cayenne pepper	**⅛ tsp**
15 g	plain flour	**½ oz**
2 tbsp	finely cut chives	**2 tbsp**
1 tbsp	chopped parsley	**1 tbsp**
	Shortcrust pastry	
175 g	plain flour	**6 oz**
⅛ tsp	salt	**⅛ tsp**
90 g	polyunsaturated margarine	**3 oz**
1	large egg, beaten	**1**

Simmer the mushrooms in the lemon juice with salt and pepper until soft. Drain in a colander set over a bowl. Pour the liquid back into the saucepan, bring to the boil, then simmer until it is reduced by half.

Meanwhile, whisk the soured cream, mustard, cayenne pepper and flour until the mixture is smooth. Stir this into the mushroom juices and cook gently, stirring constantly, until the sauce thickens. Stir in the mushrooms and the chives and remove the pan from the heat. Cover the pan and set aside to cool for about 20 minutes.

Preheat the oven to 220°C (425°F or Mark 7). Sift the flour and salt into a bowl. Rub in margarine. Reserve 1 teaspoon of the beaten egg and mix the remainder with the dry ingredients and 2 teaspoons of water to make a firm dough. Knead lightly on a floured surface until smooth.

Roll the pastry out thinly. With a plain round cutter, cut out eight rounds to line 9.5 cm (3¾ inch) fluted tartlet tins.

Fill the pastry-lined tins with the mushroom mixture. Moisten the dough strips with cold water and arrange in a lattice pattern·on the top of each tartlet. Glaze with the reserved beaten egg. Place the tartlets on a baking sheet, and bake until golden-brown—20 to 25 minutes. Serve hot sprinkled with parsley.

Middle-Eastern Spiced Carrot Salad

Serves 6

Working time: about 10 minutes

Total time: about 1 hour (includes cooling)

Calories 75
Protein 1g
Cholesterol 0mg
Total fat 5g
Saturated fat 1g
Sodium 190mg

1 kg	carrots, peeled and sliced into thick rounds	**2 lb**	**¼ tsp**	cayenne pepper	**¼ tsp**
2	garlic cloves, sliced	**2**	**2 tsp**	ground cumin	**2 tsp**
2 tbsp	virgin olive oil	**2 tbsp**	**2 tsp**	fresh lemon juice	**2 tsp**
			¼ tsp	salt	**¼ tsp**

Put the carrots and garlic into a saucepan. Cover them with hot water and boil them until they are soft—about 15 minutes. Drain the vegetables and mash them thoroughly.

In a small frying pan, heat the olive oil and fry the cayenne pepper and ground cumin for 1 minute. Stir the spice mixture into the carrot purée, mix in the lemon juice and the salt, and set the purée aside to cool at room temperature.

Spiced Fillet of Beef

Serves 12

Working time:
about 1 hour

Total time:
about 7 hours
and 30 minutes
(includes
cooling and
chilling)

Calories
290
Protein
30g
Cholesterol
65mg
Total fat
14g
Saturated fat
5g
Sodium
240mg

45 g	pine-nuts	1½ oz	1¼ tsp	salt	1¼ tsp
2 tbsp	virgin olive oil	2 tbsp	⅛ tsp	cayenne pepper	⅛ tsp
1	large onion, finely chopped	1		freshly ground black pepper	
3	garlic cloves, crushed	3	150 g	seedless raisins	5 oz
2 tsp	ground coriander	2 tsp	250 g	chestnut mushrooms, chopped	8 oz
1½ tsp	ground cardamom	1½ tsp	1.5 kg	beef fillet, trimmed	3 lb
1 tsp	ground cumin	1 tsp	2 tbsp	black peppercorns, crushed	2 tbsp
3 tsp	paprika	3 tsp	4 tbsp	finely chopped parsley	4 tbsp

Deep-fry the pine-nuts until they are lightly browned all over.

Cook the onions until soft. Add the garlic, spices, 2 teaspoons of the paprika, ¾ teaspoon of the salt, the cayenne and plenty black pepper. Cook for 2 minutes, then stir in the raisins and mushrooms. Cook for a further 10 to 15 minutes. Remove from the heat, stir in the pine-nuts and allow to cool for 30 minutes.

Preheat the oven to 220°C (425°F or Mark 7). Make an incision lengthwise through the centre of the fillet with a long, thin-bladed carving knife. Create a hole 2.5 to 5 cm (1 to 2 inches) wide and push the cooled stuffing into the hole until completely filled. Tie the fillet with string at 2.5 cm (1 inch) intervals. Season the meat with the remaining salt and coat it evenly with the crushed peppercorns.

Heat the remaining tablespoon of oil in a large, heavy roasting pan. Lightly brown the fillet on both sides, then transfer the roasting pan to the oven. Cook for 30 minutes for medium-rare meat, basting it every 10 minutes with the pan juices. For well-done meat, cook the fillet for a further 10 minutes. Let it cool at room temperature for 1 hour, then cover it with foil and chill for at least 4 hours or overnight before serving.

Ginger and Coriander Fish Balls

Makes 16
fish balls

Working time:
about 35
minutes

Total time;
about 2 hours
(includes
chilling)

Per fish ball:
Calories
70
Protein
11g
Cholesterol
25mg
Total fat
3g
Saturated fat
1g
Sodium
150mg

4 cm	fresh ginger root, grated	1½ inch	1½	egg whites, chilled	1½
3	shallots, finely chopped	3	¼ tsp	salt	¼ tsp
2 tbsp	dry vermouth	2 tbsp	1 tbsp	chopped fresh coriander	1 tbsp
1 tbsp	fresh lemon juice	1 tbsp		white pepper	
250 g	sliced smoked halibut	8 oz	2 tbsp	safflower oil	2 tbsp
500 g	fresh cod fillet, skinned, cubed and chilled	1 lb	16	small coriander sprigs	16
			1	lemon, cut into wedges	1

Simmer the ginger and shallots in a small saucepan with the vermouth and lemon juice until only half the liquid remains. Leave the mixture to cool.

Meanwhile, select the best slices of smoked halibut and cut 16 ribbons, each 7.5 by 1 cm (3 by ½ inch). Refrigerate until required.

Dice the rest of the smoked fish and chill with the ginger and shallot mixture, together with a food processor bowl and blade and a mixing bowl for at least 30 minutes. Using the chilled equipment, process the smoked fish with the cubed fresh cod, the egg whites and the salt until the mixture forms a coarse-textured ball. Transfer the ball to the bowl. Add the coriander and some white pepper,

and mix them well. Refrigerate for 30 minutes.

Pour water into a saucepan to fill it to a depth of 2.5 cm (1 inch). Line a steamer with a sheet of foil large enough to form a cover when the edges are folded over.

Divide the fish mixture into 16 portions. Roll each portion into a ball and wrap a ribbon of smoked fish around each. Arrange the balls in the steamer with the ribbon join underneath. Place a coriander sprig on top of each ball, and fold the foil over the balls.

Bring the saucepan of water to the boil. Cover the steamer and place it over the pan of boiling water. Reduce the heat and steam the balls gently for 10 to 15 minutes, until they are firm. Let cool and serve with lemon.

Mexican Beef Brochettes

Serves 4

Working time:
about 25
minutes

Total time:
about 5 hours
(includes
marinating)

Calories
250
Protein
27g
Cholesterol
55mg
Total fat
15g
Saturated fat
4g
Sodium
155mg

500 g	rump steak, in one or two slices about 1 cm (½inch) thick, trimmed of fat	**1 lb**	½ tsp	ground cumin	½ tsp
			½ tbsp	chopped fresh oregano, or ½ tsp dried oregano	½ tbsp
2	bay leaves	**2**	½ tsp	paprika	½ tsp
¼ tsp	salt	¼ tsp	½ tsp	ground cinnamon	½ tsp
	lime wedges, for garnish		**6**	cloves	**6**
	Coriander marinade		1 tbsp	sesame seeds	1 tbsp
30 g	finely chopped onion	**1 oz**	2 tbsp	finely chopped fresh coriander	2 tbsp
1	garlic clove, crushed	**1**			
1 to 2	red chili peppers, seeded and finely chopped	**1 to 2**	1½ tbsp	safflower oil	1½ tbsp
			1 tbsp	fresh lime juice	1 tbsp

Combine all the ingredients for the marinade in a shallow dish. Cut the rump steak into strips about 15 cm (6 inches) long and 6 mm (¼inch) wide, and stir them into the marinade together with the bay leaves. Cover, and put in the refrigerator to marinate for at least 4 hours, or overnight, turning once or twice. Remove the beef from the refrigerator at least 30 minutes before cooking.

Soak eight wooden skewers in water for 10 minutes. Thread the meat strips on to the skewers, sprinkling on any remaining marinade. Cook the brochettes over hot coals for 5 to 8 minutes, turning them frequently.

Transfer the brochettes to a serving plate. Sprinkle the brochettes with the salt and serve them garnished with the lime wedges.

Red Pork

Serves 4

Working time:
about 25
minutes

Total time:
about 1 hour
and 25
minutes

Calories
235
Protein
22g
Cholesterol
70mg
Total fat
15g
Saturated fat
4g
Sodium
180mg

500 g	neck end of pork, cubed	1 lb	1 tbsp	tomato paste	1 tbsp
1	lemon, juice only	1	1 tsp	ground turmeric	1 tsp
2 tbsp	safflower oil	2 tbsp	8	black peppercorns, crushed	8
1	onion, very finely chopped	1	¼tsp	coriander seeds, crushed	¼tsp
3	garlic cloves, crushed	3	¼tsp	salt	¼tsp
6	large red tomatoes,	6	8	fresh coriander sprigs, chopped	8

Put the pork into a shallow dish with the lemon juice and leave to marinate for 1 hour.

Heat the oil in a frying pan and add the onion, garlic, tomatoes and tomato paste. Cook for 3 minutes, then add the turmeric, peppercorns and pork. Cook, uncovered, for a further 3 minutes to brown the pork; to prevent burning, you may need to add about 3 tablespoons of water. Add the coriander seeds and salt, cover the pan and cook over medium heat for a further 15 minutes, until the meat is tender.

Serve in a warmed dish garnished with the chopped fresh coriander.

Mexican Pork

Serves 4

Working time:
about 20 minutes

Total time:
about 8 hours (includes soaking)

Calories
250
Protein
25g
Cholesterol
80mg
Total fat
11g
Saturated fat
4g
Sodium
290mg

500 g	pork fillet, trimmed of fat and cut into cubes	**1 lb**
60 g	dried kidney beans, soaked in water for 7 to 8 hours or overnight	**2 oz**
1 tbsp	virgin olive oil	**1 tbsp**
1	onion, finely chopped	**1**
1	garlic clove, crushed	**1**
1 tsp	chili powder	**1 tsp**
¼ tsp	ground allspice	**¼ tsp**
1½ tbsp	tomato paste	**1½ tbsp**
30 cl	unsalted chicken stock	**½ pint**
2 tsp	arrowroot	**2 tsp**
½ tsp	salt	**½ tsp**
2 tbsp	soured cream	**2 tbsp**
2 tbsp	plain low-fat yogurt	**2 tbsp**

Drain the kidney beans, place them in a saucepan, cover with water and bring to the boil. Boil rapidly for at least 10 minutes, then reduce the heat, cover and simmer until tender. Drain well.

Heat the oil in a large heavy saucepan; add the pork, onion and garlic and cook for 4 to 5 minutes, stirring frequently to brown.

Stir in the chili powder, allspice and tomato paste; add the stock. Bring to the boil, then reduce the heat, cover and simmer for 20 minutes.

Add the cooked kidney beans to the pan. In a small bowl, mix the arrowroot with 2 tablespoons of cold water. Add the mixture to the pan and stir well, until the juices are thickened. Season with the salt.

Mix together the soured cream and yogurt. Spoon a quarter of the mixture on to each serving.

Kofta with Curry Sauce and Cucumber

<table>
<tr><td>Serves 8</td></tr>
<tr><td>Working (and total) time: about 55 minutes</td></tr>
</table>

Calories	230
Protein	22g
Cholesterol	65mg
Total fat	11g
Saturated fat	3g
Sodium	275mg

750 g	trimmed leg or neck end of pork, minced	1½ lb
¼ tsp	chili powder	¼ tsp
1½ tsp	ground turmeric	1½ tsp
1 tsp	ground cardamom	1 tsp
⅛ tsp	salt	½ tsp
1 cm	piece fresh ginger root, chopped	½ inch
2 tbsp	besan flour or soya flour	2 tbsp
2 tsp	coriander, finely chopped	2 tsp
1 tsp	parsley prigs, chopped	1 tsp
250 g	cucumber, cubed	8 oz

	Curry sauce	
2 tbsp	safflower oil	2 tbsp
250 g	onions, very finely chopped	8 oz
1	garlic clove, crushed	1
2.5 cm	piece cinnamon stick	1 inch
4	cloves	4
2 tbsp	ground coriander and cumin	2 tbsp
¼ tsp	chili powder	¼ tsp
1	bay leaf	1
½ tsp	salt .	½ tsp
250 g	potatoes, grated	8 oz
500 g	tomatoes, skinned, seeded	1 lb

For the sauce, preheat a large browning dish for 5 to 7 minutes. Add the oil and onion and microwave on high, stirring occasionally, until the onions are softened. Stir in the garlic, spices, chili powder, bay leaf and salt, and microwave on high for 30 seconds. Add the potatoes, tomatoes and 45 cl (¾ pint) of water; cover and cook on high for 20 minutes, stirring occasionally.

While the sauce cooks, mix the chili powder, turmeric, cardamom, salt, ginger and flour, add the chopped coriander and parsley, and mix together. Shape the mixture into 16 balls and set them aside.

Purée and sieve the cooked sauce. Arrange the kofta in the sauce, cover and microwave on high for 5 minutes. Rearrange the kofta, baste with the sauce and microwave on high for 2 minutes, then add the cucumber pieces and cook for 1 minute more.

Spiced Chili Beef with Yogurt

Serves 4

Working time: about 1 hour and 15 minutes

Total time: about 3 hours and 30 minutes

Calories 295
Protein 40g
Cholesterol 95mg
Total fat 12g
Saturated fat 6g
Sodium 265mg

600 g	topside of beef, cubed	1¼ lb	2 tsp	ground turmeric	2 tsp
6	cardamom pods	6	500 g	tomatoes, skinned, chopped	1 lb
2 tsp	coriander seeds	2 tsp	¼ tsp	salt	¼ tsp
2 tsp	cumir seeds	2 tsp	17.5 cl	plain low-fat yogurt	6 fl oz
30 g	ghee or clarified butter,	1 oz		(at room temperature)	
1	medium onion, chopped	1	½	small sweet red pepper,	½
2	garlic cloves, crushed	2		sliced into rings	
	green chili peppers, chopped		½	small sweet green pepper,	½
2.5 cm	fresh ginger root, crushed	1 inch		sliced into rings	

Split the cardamom pods open and remove the seeds. Gently dry-fry with the coriander and cumin seeds until the seeds give off a spicy aroma. Remove from the pan and crush.

Melt half the ghee or butter in a casserole and add the beef in batches. Brown, then drain and dry.

Lower the heat and add the onion, garlic, chili peppers and ginger to the casserole, stirring. Cook gently, stirring constantly, until softened. Meanwhile, preheat the oven to 150°C (300°F or Mark 2).

Add the crushed spices and turmeric, and cook, stirring, for 2 minutes. Increase the heat, then add the tomatoes and salt, and cook, stirring, for 5 minutes. Return the beef to the casserole and stir well.

Reserve about 3 tablespoons of yogurt. Slowly add the rest to the casserole. Stir-fry after each addition until it is absorbed before adding more. Cover the casserole with foil and a lid. Cook in the oven for 2 hours until the meat is tender, stirring occasionally.

Just before serving, melt the remaining ghee or butter in a heavy frying pan, add the pepper rings and toss until softened slightly. Drain on paper towels. Top with the pepper rings and reserved yogurt. Serve hot.

Haddock Enchiladas with Chili Sauce

Serves 4

Working (and total) time about 1 hour

Calories
400
Protein
23g
Cholesterol
50mg
Total fat
9g
Saturated fat
1g
Sodium
295mg

350 g	haddock fillets	**12 oz**
90 g	long-grain rice	**3 oz**
1	dried hot chili pepper, chopped	**1**
¼ tsp	salt	**¼ tsp**
	freshly ground black pepper	
2 tbsp	safflower oil	**2 tbsp**
1	garlic clove, finely chopped	**1**
1	small onion, finely chopped	**1**
750 g	ripe tomatoes, skinned, seeded and chopped	**1½ lb**

12.5 cl	fish stock or white wine	**4 fl oz**
¼ tsp	ground cumin	**¼ tsp**
8	corn tortillas	**8**
	Chili sauce	
500 g	green tomatoes, skinned, seeded and chopped	**1 lb**
1	fresh hot chili pepper, chopped	**1**
2 tbsp	chopped fresh coriander	**2 tbsp**
1	small onion, finely chopped	**1**
	freshly ground black pepper	

Preheat the oven to 190°C (375°F or Mark 5). In a 1 litre (2 pint) casserole, combine the rice, dried chili pepper, ¼ teaspoon of the salt and 30 cl (½ pint) of water. Boil, cover and cook until the rice is tender.

Put the green tomatoes in a saucepan with 8 cl (3 fl oz) of water and simmer for 5 minutes. Drain, then put them in a blender with the chili pepper, coriander, onion and some black pepper, and blend to a coarse purée. Rinse the fillets, pat dry and season.

Heat the oil in a large, heavy frying pan over medium heat. Add the garlic and cook for 30 seconds, stirring constantly. Add the onion, the tomatoes with the fish stock or wine, the cumin and the pepper and simmer. Add the fish and simmer until it can be broken into small pieces. Spoon the rice in and stir.

To assemble the enchiladas, gently heat a small frying pan and place a tortilla in the pan to heat for 30 seconds. With each tortilla add 6 tablespoons of fish mixture in a straight line and roll it up. Then place the enchilada in an oiled casserole with the seam side down. Pour the chili sauce over the enchiladas and warm in the oven. Serve immediately.

Chili and Lime Avocado Dip

Serves 12

Working time:
about 15
minutes

Total time:
about 3 hours
and 15
minutes

Calories
105
Protein
2g
Cholesterol
0mg
Total fat
11g
Saturated fat
1g
Sodium
35mg

4	ripe avocados	4	1	spring onion, finely chopped	1
1 tbsp	fresh lime juice	1 tbsp	1 tbsp	finely chopped	1 tbsp
1 tbsp	virgin olive oil	1 tbsp		fresh coriander	
1	pickled green chili, chopped	1	¼ tsp	salt	¼ tsp
1	garlic clove, crushed	1		freshly ground black pepper	

Cut the avocados in half and spoon the flesh into a bowl. Mash lightly with a fork—the texture should not be too smooth. Stir in the lime juice and oil, then the chili, garlic, spring onion, coriander, salt and some pepper. Cover the mixture and set aside for at least 3 hours in order to allow the chili to permeate the dip. Serve at room temperature.

Spicy Chicken Wings

Makes 24 pieces

Working time: about 30 minutes

Total time: about 5 hours (includes marinating

Per piece:
Calories 15
Protein 2g
Cholesterol 10mg
Total fat trace
Saturated fat trace
Sodium 45mg

12	chicken wings	**12**
15 cl	plain low-fat yogurt	**¼ pint**
1 tbsp	fresh lemon juice	**1 tbsp**
1 tbsp	honey	**1 tbsp**
2.5 cm	fresh ginger root, grated	**1 inch**
1 tsp	ground turmeric	**1 tsp**
1 tbsp	boemboe sesate, or ¾ tsp each ground coriander, cumin, galangal and lemon grass	**1 tbsp**
½ tsp	salt	**½ tsp**
	curly endive or lettuce, for garnish	

Cut off the chicken wing tips, and either discard or reserve them for stock-making. Separate each wing into two at the joint, and trim off loose skin with scissors or a sharp knife.

Combine the yogurt, lemon juice, honey, ginger, turmeric, boemboe sesate and salt, and spread the mixture over the chicken pieces. Leave to marinate in a cool place for at least 4 hours, preferably overnight. Preheat the oven to 230°C (450°F or Mark 8).

Remove the chicken pieces from the marinade and arrange them in a baking dish or ovenproof casserole. Bake the chicken in the oven for about 15 minutes. Serve slightly cooled, for ease of handling, on a bed of curly endive or a chiffonade of lettuce.

Editor's Note: The chicken pieces may also be cooked under a hot grill, turning at least once until they are well browned—about 15 minutes.

Curry Fettuccine with Chicken and Avocado

Serves 6		
Working time: about 45 minutes		
Total time: about 2 hours and 15 minutes		

Calories 360		
Protein 25g		
Cholesterol 95mg		
Total fat 14g		
Saturated fat 2g		
Sodium 480mg		

250 g	fettucine	80 oz	500 g	chicken breasts, boned	1 lb
¼ litre	plain low-fat yogurt	8 fl oz	½	avocado, peeled and cubed	½
¾ tsp	curry powder	¾ tsp	350 g	carrots, peeled and cubed	12 oz
¼ tsp	salt	¼ tsp		freshly ground black pepper	
1	garlic clove, crushed	1	2 tbsp	safflower oil	2 tbsp
5 tbsp	fresh lemon juice	5 tbsp	2 tbsp	finely chopped parsley	2 tbsp

In a large, shallow bowl, combine half the yogurt, ¼ teaspoon of the curry powder, ¼ teaspoon of the salt, the garlic and 3 tablespoons of the lemon juice. Lay the chicken in the bowl and spoon the yogurt mixture over them. Marinate in the refrigerator for at least 2 hours, turning every 30 minutes.

Put the avocado cubes in a small bowl. Pour the remaining 2 tablespoons of lemon juice over them, then toss the cubes gently to coat them. Set aside.

Boil the carrots in water until tender. In a blender purée the carrots with their reserved cooking liquid. Add the remaining yogurt and curry powder, and purée again. Transfer the

mixture to a small saucepan and warm it over low heat.

Meanwhile, wipe the marinade from the chicken breasts and discard it. Sprinkle the chicken with some pepper. Heat the oil in a heavy frying pan over medium-high heat. Add the chicken breasts to the pan and sauté them until they are cooked through—4 to 5 minutes on each side. Cut the meat into chunks; cover the chunks and set them aside in a warm place.

Cook the fettucine in salted boiling water until it is *al dente*.

Arrange the purée, fettucine, chicken and advocado together as illustrated, garnish with parsley.

Chicken with Orange and Onion

Serves 8

Working time:
about 30
minutes

Total time:
about 1 hour
and 15
minutes

Calories
370
Protein
42g
Cholesterol
125mg
Total fat
14g
Saturated fat
3g
Sodium
255mg

2 x 1.5 kg	chickens, wings removed quartered and skinned	2 x 3 lb	3	onions, thinly sliced	3
2 tbsp	flour	2 tbsp	2 tsp	fresh thyme, or	2 tsp
½ tsp	salt	½ tsp		½ tsp dried thyme	
	freshly ground black pepper		30 cl	fresh orange juice	½ pint
2 tbsp	safflower oil	2 tbsp	2 tbsp	fresh lemon juice	2 tbsp
1	orange, rind only, julienned	1	1 tbsp	honey	1 tbsp
			17.5 cl	dry white wine	6 fl oz

Dust the chicken pieces with the flour. Sprinkle them with ¼ teaspoon of the salt and some of the pepper.

In a large, heavy frying pan, heat the oil over medium-high heat and sauté the chicken in several batches until golden-brown—about 5 minutes on each side. Transfer the pieces to a 23 by 33 cm (9 by 13 inch) baking dish and scatter the orange rind over them.

Preheat the oven to 180°C (350°F or Mark 4). Over medium-low heat, cook the onions in the oil in the pan, stirring occasionally, until they are translucent—about 10 minutes. Stir in the thyme and the remaining salt and spread the mixture over the chicken pieces.

Pour the orange and lemon juice, honey and wine into the pan. Bring the liquid to the boil and reduce it to about ¼ litre (8 fl oz). Pour the liquid over the chicken. Cook the pieces uncovered in the oven, basting once with the liquid, until the juices run clear when a thigh is pierced with the tip of a sharp knife—about 35 minutes.

Leg of Lamb in Spiced Apple Sauce

Serves 12

Working time: about 45 minutes

Total time: about 2 hours and 25 minutes

Calories 225

Protein 30g

Cholesterol 80mg

Total fat 9g

Saturated fat 4g

Sodium 135mg

2.5 kg	leg of lamb, trimmed and boned	**5 lb**
4 tbsp	cider vinegar	**4 tbsp**
1	onion, finely chopped	**1**
2	garlic cloves, finely chopped	**2**
1 tbsp	finely chopped fresh sage	**1 tbsp**
½ tsp	salt	**½ tsp**
1 tbsp	freshly ground black pepper	**1 tbsp**

1 tbsp	safflower oil	**1 tbsp**
	Spiced apple sauce	
300 g	cooking apples, peeled, cored and sliced	**10 oz**
30 g	sugar	**1 oz**
2	cloves	**2**
¼ tsp	ground cinnamon	**¼ tsp**
⅛ tsp	ground allspice	**⅛ tsp**

Cook the apples gently in a heavy saucepan with 1 tablespoon of water, until they are soft. Drain and purée by pressing them through a sieve. Return the purée to the pan, add the sugar and spices, and gently cook, stirring occasionally, until the mixture has a thick spreading consistency. Remove the cloves and set aside to cool.

Spread the lamb flat on a work surface with the cut side facing upwards. Cut out the membranes and tendons and discard. Starting from the centre of the meat, slice horizontally into the flesh at one side of the leg, making sure that you do not cut completely through.

Open out the resulting flap, then slice into the opposite side and open it out in a similar manner.

Put the apple sauce into a large bowl and mix in the vinegar, onion, garlic, sage, salt, pepper and oil. Put the lamb into the bowl and spread the apple sauce mixture thickly all over it. Marinate at room temperature for about 1 hour, turning it after 30 minutes.

Preheat the grill for 10 minutes. Remove the lamb from the marinade and cook for 12 minutes on each side for medium-rare meat. Baste with the reserved marinade. Rest the lamb for about 15 minutes, then carve and serve.

Moussaka

Serves 6

Working time
about 1 hour
and
10 minutes

Total time:
about 2 hours
and
30 minutes

Calories
380
Protein
30g
Cholesterol
90mg
Total fat
14g
Saturated fat
6g
Sodium
370mg

500 g	lean lamb, minced	**1 lb**
2	onions, chopped	**2**
2	garlic cloves	**2**
500 g	ripe tomatoes, chopped	**1 lb**
20 cl	red wine	**7 fl oz**
2 tbsp	tomato paste	**2 tbsp**
1	green chili pepper, chopped	**1**
2 tbsp	chopped parsley	**2 tbsp**
1 tbsp	chopped fresh marjoram	**1 tbsp**
1	bay leaf	**1**
¼ tsp	freshly grated nutmeg	**¼ tsp**

¾ tsp	salt	**¾ tsp**
	freshly ground black pepper	
750 g	aubergines, thinly sliced	**1½ lb**
250 g	potatoes, thinly sliced	**8 oz**
30 g	Parmesan cheese, grated	**1 oz**
	White sauce	
60 g	polyunsaturated margarine	**2 oz**
60 g	plain flour	**2 oz**
30 cl	skimmed milk	**½ pint**
½ tsp	freshly grated nutmeg	**½ tsp**
30 cl	plain low-fat yogurt	**½ pint**

Lightly brush a frying pan with oil and gently heat. Brown the minced lamb, add the onions and continue stirring for a further 5 minutes. Add the garlic, tomatoes, wine, tomato paste, chili and herbs and bring to the boil, then cover and simmer gently for 40 minutes.

Meanwhile, sprinkle the aubergine slices with the remaining ½ teaspoon of salt. Leave them to stand for 20 minutes. Steam the aubergines until tender—about 10 minutes. While they are steaming, boil the potato slices until tender—about 5 minutes. Drain well.

Preheat the oven to 180°C (350°F or Mark 4). Layer the bottom of a baking dish with the potato slices, then half the aubergines, the meat mixture, and remaining aubergine on top.

Melt the margarine in a saucepan, add the flour and stir for 1 minute. Gradually stir in the milk, the nutmeg and the salt until it thickens. Let cool and stir in the yogurt. Pour over the moussaka, sprinkle on the Parmesan and bake until golden-brown. Serve hot.

Spicy Beef Salad

Serves 4

Working time:
about 25
minutes

Total time:
about 2 hours
45 minutes
(includes
marinating)

Calories
295
Protein
22g
Cholesterol
55mg
Total fat
5g
Saturated fat
2g
Sodium
120mg

500 g	sirloin steak in one piece	1 lb
8	whole cloves	8
8	black peppercorns	8
12	allspice berries	12
1	large onion, thinly sliced	1
2 tbsp	brandy	2 tbsp
½ litre	red wine	16 fl oz

175 g	mixed dried fruit, chopped	6 oz
4 tbsp	red wine vinegar	4 tbsp
1	cinnamon stick	1
500 g	turnips, peeled, halved lengthwise and sliced	1 lb
4 tbsp	chopped parsley	4 tbsp
	several watercress sprigs	

Put the steak into a shallow pan with the cloves, peppercorns, allspice berries, onion slices, brandy and ¼ litre (8 fl oz) of the wine. Marinate at room temperature for 2 hours, turning now and again. In a saucepan, combine the dried fruit with the vinegar, the remaining wine, ¼ litre (8 fl oz) of water and the cinnamon stick. Bring to the boil, then lower the heat, and simmer the mixture for 30 minutes. Drain the fruit in a sieve set over a bowl, discard the cinnamon stick and set the fruit aside. Return the liquid to the saucepan and boil it until it is reduced by about half.

Preheat the oven to 240°C (475°F or Mark 9). Pour enough water into a saucepan to fill it about 2.5 cm (1 inch) deep. Set a vegetable steamer in the pan and bring the water to the boil. Put the turnips into the steamer, cover the pan, and steam the turnips until they are tender—about 10 minutes. Transfer the turnips to a bowl and set them aside.

Remove the steak from the marinade and pat it dry with paper towels; discard the marinade. Roast the steak for 15 minutes, then remove it from the oven, and let it rest for 30 minutes. Cut the steak against the grain into slices and cut each slice into strips.

Toss the beef with the wine mixture, parsley, turnips and the fruit. Arrange on a platter; garnish it with watercress and serve.

Lamb Paprika

Serves 4

Working time:
about 25
minutes

Total time:
about 6 hours
and 25 minutes
(includes
marinating)

Calories
245
Protein
30g
Cholesterol
85mg
Total fat
11g
Saturated fat
5g
Sodium
350mg

500 g	lean lamb trimmed and cut into thin strips	1 lb		15 g	polyunsaturated margarine	½ oz
1 tbsp	paprika	1 tbsp		1	garlic clove, crushed	1
¼ tsp	freshly ground black pepper	¼ tsp		3	shallots, thinly sliced	3
½ tsp	salt	½ tsp		2	bay leaves	2
350 g	kale, washed, stemmed and chopped	12 oz		3	tomatoes, skinned and chopped	3
2 tsp	caraway seeds	2 tsp		3 tbsp	medium-dry sherry	3 tbsp
				2 tbsp	soured cream	2 tbsp

Put the lamb in a bowl with the paprika, the pepper and half of the salt, and stir until the meat is evenly coated. Cover the bowl and leave it in a cool place to marinate for at least 6 hours or overnight. Stir the meat once during this period.

Pour enough water into a large saucepan to fill it about 2.5 cm (1 inch) deep. Place a vegetable steamer in the pan and bring the water to the boil. Put the chopped kale in the steamer and sprinkle it with the remaining salt and the caraway seeds. Cover the saucepan and cook until the kale is just tender and bright green—5 to 6 minutes.

Meanwhile, melt the margarine in a large, heavy frying pan. Stir in the garlic, shallots and bay leaves and cook them over medium heat until the shallots are softened—1 to 2 minutes. Increase the heat to high and sauté the lamb, stirring occasionally, until it has changed colour all over—2 to 3 minutes. Stir in the tomatoes and sherry. Bring the mixture to the boil and cook it for 2 minutes.

Spoon the kale into a hot serving dish, cover it and keep it warm. Transfer the lamb and its sauce to a second hot dish, stir in the soured cream and serve immediately, accompanied by the kale.

Barbecued Veal with Spicy Orange Sauce

Serves 8

Working time:
about 1 hour

Total time:
about 3 hours
(includes
marinating)

Calories
230
Protein
22g
Cholesterol
90mg
Total fat
10g
Saturated fat
3g
Sodium
160mg

1 kg	veal rump, trimmed	2 lb
1 tsp	allspice	1 tsp
1 tsp	juniper berries	1 tsp
2 tbsp	virgin olive oil	2 tbsp
¼ tsp	salt	¼ tsp
	freshly ground black pepper	
2	orange rind, finely grated	2
	Spicy orange sauce	
¼ litre	fresh orange juice	8 fl oz

4 tbsp	clear honey	4 tbsp
2 tbsp	red wine vinegar	2 tbsp
2	garlic cloves, crushed	2
400 g	canned tomatoes, drained	14 oz
1 tbsp	Grand Marnier	1 tbsp
½ tsp	paprika	½ tsp
	Tabasco sauce	
¼ tsp	salt	¼ tsp
	freshly ground black pepper	

To prepare the marinade, crush the allspice and juniper berries together with a pestle and mortar, then blend in the oil, salt, some pepper and the grated orange rind.

Place the veal joint in a shallow dish, pour the marinade over it and coat well. Cover and marinate at room temperature for 2 to 3 hours.

To prepare the sauce, put the orange juice, honey, wine vinegar, garlic, tomatoes and Grand Marnier in a heavy-bottomed saucepan. Add the paprika, a few drops of Tabasco sauce, the salt and some pepper. Bring to the boil, then lower the heat and

simmer very gently for 45 minutes to 1 hour, until the sauce is reduced and thickened.

Light the charcoal in the barbecue about 30 minutes before cooking time. Skewer the veal into a neat shape using one or two large skewers. Cook on a rack over hot, but not fierce, coals, turning frequently until cooked through but still slightly pink inside—35 to 45 minutes—taking care that the veal does not burn.

To serve, carefully slide the veal off the skewers on to a cutting board then cut into thin slices. Serve with the spicy orange sauce.

Hamburgers with Spicy Pumpkin Ketchup

Serves 8

Working time: about 15 minutes

Total time: about 1 hour and 15 minutes

Calories
275

Protein
21g

Cholesterol
45mg

Total fat
5g

Saturated fat
2g

Sodium
155mg

850 g	beef topside, minced	1¾ lb	2.5 cl	cider vinegar	4 fl oz
225 g	borghul	7½ oz	2 tbsp	sugar	2 tbsp
2	garlic cloves	2	2 tsp	honey	2 tsp
25 g	parsley, chopped	1 oz	½ tsp	ground cloves	½ tsp
2 tbsp	grainy mustard	2 tbsp	½ tsp	curry powder	½ tsp
	Spicy Pumpkin ketchup		¼ tsp	ground allspice	¼ tsp
500 g	canned pumpkin	1 lb	¼ tsp	cayenne pepper	¼ tsp
1	onion, chopped	1	¼ tsp	salt	¼ tsp
1	apple or pear, chopped	1		freshly ground black pepper	

Combine the ketchup ingredients in a saucepan. Stir in   litre (8 fl oz) of water and simmer the mixture gently for 1 hour. Purée the ketchup in a blender, then work through a sieve with a wooden spoon. Set aside.

Put the burghul into a heatproof bowl and pour 40 cl (13 fl oz) of boiling water over it.

Cover the bowl and leave for 30 minutes. Preheat the grill for ten minutes.

Put the minced beef, burghul, garlic, parsley and mustard into a bowl, and combine them by hand. Form eight patties and grill for 3 to 4 minutes on each side for medium-rare meat. Serve hot.

Spit-Roasted Savoury Chicken

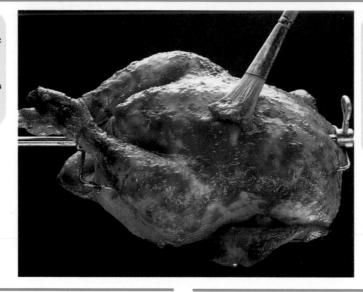

Serves 8

Working time: about 35 minutes

Total time: about 7 hours (includes marinating)

Calories 195
Protein 24g
Cholesterol 90mg
Total fat 9g
Saturated fat 2g
Sodium 85mg

2 tbsp	safflower oil	2 tbsp
1	small onion, grated	1
500 g	tomatoes, skinned, seeded, and chopped	1 lb
½	lemon, strained juice only	½
2 tbsp	Worcester sauce	2 tbsp
1 tsp	Tabasco sauce	1 tsp
1 tsp	dry mustard	1 tsp
2 tbsp	dark brown sugar	2 tbsp
1.75 kg	roasting chicken	3½ lb

Heat the oil in a heavy saucepan over low heat. Add the onion and cook for 2 minutes, until it is softened but not browned. Stir in the tomatoes, lemon juice, Worcester sauce, Tabasco sauce, mustard and sugar. Cover the pan and simmer the ingredients for 15 minutes, stirring occasionally, until the tomatoes are reduced to a purée. Remove the pan from the heat and pour the marinade into a bowl, then set it aside until it is cool.

Put the chicken in a large bowl and pour on the marinade. Cover the bowl and leave the chicken to marinate for at least 4 hours, at room temperature, turning it several times.

Push a barbecue spit rod into the marinated chicken through the neck flap just above the breast bone, and out just above the tail. Secure the spit rod with the holding forks and attach the spit to the barbecue, on the turning mechanism. Rearrange the coals to leave room for a drip tray immediately below the chicken; set the drip tray in place.

Cook the chicken for 1¼ to 1½ hours, or until it is tender and the juices run clear when a thigh is pierced with a skewer. Baste the chicken frequently while it is cooking, first with the marinade, then with the cooking juices from the drip tray.

Yogurt Chicken Drumsticks

Serves 8

Working time:
about 30
minutes

Total time:
about 3 hours
and 30 minutes
(includes
marinating)

Calories
160
Protein
26g
Cholesterol
90mg
Total fat
6g
Saturated fat
2g
Sodium
190mg

16	chicken drumsticks (about 1.5 kg/3 lb), skinned	**16**	**½ tsp**	Tabasco sauce	**½ tsp**
½ tsp	salt	**½ tsp**	**15 cl**	plain low-fat yogurt	**½ pint**
1	lemon, grated rind and juice	**1**		freshly ground black pepper	
3 tbsp	paprika	**3 tbsp**		crisp salad leaves, for garnish	

Cut two deep, diagonal slits in opposite sides of each drumstick. In a small bowl, stir the salt and the grated lemon rind into the lemon juice, then rub the mixture over each drumstick and into the slits. Place the drumsticks on a wire rack set over a baking tray, and sieve 1 tablespoon of the paprika evenly over the upper side of the drumsticks.

In another bowl, mix together the Tabasco sauce, yogurt and some black pepper. Using a brush, coat the paprika-sprinkled side of each drumstick with the yogurt mixture. Turn the drumsticks over, sieve another tablespoon of paprika over them, and coat them with the remaining yogurt mixture. Set the drumsticks aside for 3 hours, until the yogurt begins to dry.

Lightly oil the barbecue rack. Cook the drumsticks over hot coals for 15 to 20 minutes, turning them every 5 minutes. After the last turn, sprinkle the remaining paprika over the drumsticks. Serve the drumsticks immediately, garnished with crisp salad leaves.

Useful weights and measures

Weight Equivalents

Avoirdupois		Metric
1 ounce	=	28.35 grams
1 pound	=	254.6 grams
2.3 pounds	=	1 kilogram

Liquid Measurements

$^1/_4$ pint	=	$1^1/_2$ decilitres
$^1/_2$ pint	=	$^1/_4$ litre
scant 1 pint	=	$^1/_2$ litre
$1^3/_4$ pints	=	1 litre
1 gallon	=	4.5 litres

Liquid Measures

1 pint	=	20 fl oz	=	32 tablespoons
$^1/_2$ pint	=	10 fl oz	=	16 tablespoons
$^1/_4$ pint	=	5 fl oz	=	8 tablespoons
$^1/_8$ pint	=	$2^1/_2$ fl oz	=	4 tablespoons
$^1/_{16}$ pint	=	$1^1/_4$ fl oz	=	2 tablespoons

Solid Measures

1 oz almonds, ground = $3^3/_4$ level tablespoons
1 oz breadcrumbs fresh = 7 level tablespoons
1 oz butter, lard = 2 level tablespoons
1 oz cheese, grated = $3^1/_2$ level tablespoons
1 oz cocoa = $2^3/_4$ level tablespoons
1 oz desiccated coconut = $4^1/_2$ tablespoons
1 oz cornflour = $2^1/_2$ tablespoons
1 oz custard powder = $2^1/_2$ tablespoons
1 oz curry powder and spices = 5 tablespoons
1 oz flour = 2 level tablespoons
1 oz rice, uncooked = $1^1/_2$ tablespoons
1 oz sugar, caster and granulated = 2 tablespoons
1 oz icing sugar = $2^1/_2$ tablespoons
1 oz yeast, granulated = 1 level tablespoon

American Measures

16 fl oz	=1 American pint
8 fl oz	=1 American standard cup
0.50 fl oz	=1 American tablespoon

(slightly smaller than British Standards Institute tablespoon)

0.16 fl oz	=1 American teaspoon

Australian Cup Measures
(Using the 8-liquid-ounce cup measure)

1 cup flour	4 oz
1 cup sugar (crystal or caster)	8 oz
1 cup icing sugar (free from lumps)	5 oz
1 cup shortening (butter, margarine)	8 oz
1 cup brown sugar (lightly packed)	4 oz
1 cup soft breadcrumbs	2 oz
1 cup dry breadcrumbs	3 oz
1 cup rice (uncooked)	6 oz
1 cup rice (cooked)	5 oz
1 cup mixed fruit	4 oz
1 cup grated cheese	4 oz
1 cup nuts (chopped)	4 oz
1 cup coconut	$2^1/_2$ oz

Australian Spoon Measures

	level tablespoon
1 oz flour	2
1 oz sugar	$1^1/_2$
1 oz icing sugar	2
1 oz shortening	1
1 oz honey	1
1 oz gelatine	2
1 oz cocoa	3
1 oz cornflour	$2^1/_2$
1 oz custard powder	$2^1/_2$

Australian Liquid Measures
(Using 8-liquid-ounce cup)

1 cup liquid	8 oz
$2^1/_2$ cups liquid	20 oz (1 pint)
2 tablespoons liquid	1 oz
1 gill liquid	5 oz ($^1/_4$ pint)